## Praise for *The Workplace You Need Now*

"Technology will increasingly play an important role to help measure, model, and manage a connected, sustainable workplace."

—**Brad Smith,**
**President, Microsoft**

"The opportunities to transform work and workplaces are staring us in the face. The dynamics of change described in this book make it a must-read for all that want to create a culture for the success of their organizations."

—**Rajesh Nambiar,**
**Chairman, Cognizant India**

"Must-read for anyone who wants to understand the new world of work."

—**Philip Ross,**
**Founder and CEO, UnWork.com**

"Now is the time for companies to leverage the power of design to transform the human experience at work. We see first-hand the challenges and opportunities companies face in this new era of the office. This book is a refreshing and readable narrative that reinforces human-centric design."

—**Diane Hoskins,**
**Co-CEO, Gensler**

"The most successful workplaces will embody and exemplify an organization's purpose, inspire the workforce, and drive business performance. The book is an invaluable guide for CEOs thinking about the future of work and the workplaces they need to help their people and businesses thrive."

—**Christian Ulbrich,**
**CEO and President, JLL**

"Technologies constantly change the workplace experience and the real estate sector's ability to respond. For those that need to motivate and change, this book captures the factors that are critical to understand the hybrid future of work in our ever digitizing and virtual culture."

**—Dr. Andrea Chegut,**
**Director, MIT Real Estate Innovation Lab**

# THE
# WORKPLACE
# YOU NEED
# NOW

SANJAY RISHI
BENJAMIN BRESLAU
PETER MISCOVICH

# THE
# WORKPLACE
# YOU NEED
# NOW

SHAPING SPACES FOR
THE **FUTURE OF WORK**

WILEY

Published by John Wiley & Sons, Inc., Hoboken, New Jersey.
Published simultaneously in Canada.

For general information on our other products and services or for technical support, please contact our Customer Care Department within the United States at (800) 762-2974, outside the United States at (317) 572-3993, or fax (317) 572-4002.

Wiley publishes in a variety of print and electronic formats and by print-on-demand. Some material included with standard print versions of this book may not be included in ebooks or in print-on-demand. If this book refers to media such as a CD or DVD that is not included in the version you purchased, you may download this material at http://booksupport.wiley.com. For more information about Wiley products, visit www.wiley.com.

*Library of Congress Cataloging-in-Publication Data*
Names: Rishi, Sanjay, author. | Breslau, Benjamin, author. | Miscovich,
   Peter, author.
Title: The workplace you need now : shaping spaces for the future of work /
   Sanjay Rishi, Benjamin Breslau, Peter Miscovich.
Description: Hoboken, New Jersey : John Wiley & Sons, Inc., [2022] |
   Includes index.
Identifiers: LCCN 2021038320 (print) | LCCN 2021038321 (ebook) | ISBN
   9781119814801 (cloth) | ISBN 9781119815136 (adobe pdf) | ISBN
   9781119815129 (epub)
Subjects: LCSH: Work environment. | Office layout. | Office buildings. |
   Flexible work arrangements. | Organizational change. | Organizational
   effectiveness.
Classification: LCC HD7261 .R4968 2021 (print) | LCC HD7261 (ebook) | DDC
   658.2/3—dc23
LC record available at https://lccn.loc.gov/2021038320
LC ebook record available at https://lccn.loc.gov/2021038321

Cover Design: Wiley
Author Photos: © JLL Americas

SKY10029952_092321

*To the perfection in my life – my wife, Neha,
and our children, Natasha, Sumit, and Shivani. To the
priceless little treasure, Sanjana! And to Dad, Mom –
the force of nature for her boys – my brother Girish,
and our enriching weekend banters!*

—Sanjay Rishi


*To my wife, Edie; my children, Sam, Emma, and Jack;
my parents, Susan and Bill Breslau; my brother, Jeremy;
and all my family, friends, and colleagues who support
and inspire me every day.*

—Ben Breslau


*To honor and in loving memory of our father,
John A. Miscovich; to our amazing mother,
Mary Miscovich; and with heartfelt dedication to my
wonderful partner of 31 years, Damon Owen.*

—Peter Miscovich

# CONTENTS

*Preface*                                                                                    *xi*

*Introduction*                                                                               *xv*

**PART I**      **The Personalized Workplace**                                               **1**

**Chapter 1**   The Origin and Evolution of Workplace                                        5

**Chapter 2**   Personalizing the Workplace                                                  19

**Chapter 3**   The Future Is Flexible                                                       41

**PART II**     **The Responsible Workplace**                                                **63**

**Chapter 4**   The Purpose-Driven Workplace                                                 67

**Chapter 5**   The New Corporate Responsibility                                             77

**Chapter 6**   A Resilient Workforce, Workplace, and Portfolio                              99

**PART III**    **The Experiential Workplace**                                               **107**

**Chapter 7**   The Human Experience in the Corporate Office                                 113

**Chapter 8**   Experience in the Intelligent Digital +
                Physical Space                                                               131

**PART IV**    **The Path Forward**                                    **151**

**Chapter 9**   Reimagining the Workplace: How?                  155

**Chapter 10** Strategic Framework: Journey to The
              Hybrid Workplace                                   181

*Acknowledgments*                                               *199*

*About the Authors*                                             *203*

*Index*                                                         *205*

# PREFACE

From climate change to the COVID-19 pandemic, crises, and mass disruption – the likes of which we have experienced in past eras – we have seen devastating and yet fundamentally transformative consequences emerge. Across history, crises have catalyzed innovation and business model transformation, and have been followed by a sense of optimism. The idea for this book first emerged just as the world had been turned upside down by the COVID-19 pandemic and hopes of a quick recovery had been lost. For months, humanity reeled with uncertainty, fears, grief, and loss, and socioeconomic challenges that, combined, more closely resembled a gripping science fiction movie than real life. From dining with friends or cheering at a baseball game to taking a child to school and heading to the office, normalcy was displaced.

In the aftermath of all that despair, however, optimism, innovation, and an acceleration of lasting changes have emerged. CEOs of world-leading organizations have been on the news talking about their workplaces. The evolution of work – a perpetual journey – has become front and center as organizations begin to reconcile priorities of collaboration and culture with the learnings and implications of mass remote working. The idea of "workplace" as we knew it has undergone unprecedented and unplanned transformation.

Traditionally, of course, the office has had a central role in the business of work. "Going to work" meant going to a downtown high-rise office building or a suburban corporate campus, not your guest bedroom or kitchen table or, if you are fortunate, an actual home office. The pandemic shattered these conventional views of work and the office, and upended many other societal norms along the way.

Employee expectations shifted significantly during the pandemic, as many continued to be just as productive from home as in the office – and they didn't miss the commute. Many organizations are now shifting their expectations, examining their workplaces and real estate portfolios as they ponder the evolving purpose their workplaces should serve.

The value of the workplace is being redefined, with the recognition that brand, talent, culture, and creativity are inherently intertwined. Enterprises large and small, public and private, along with communities, are assessing whether the current shifts we are seeing in how people live and work are cyclical or structural. Consumers are adopting new lifestyles and rethinking their value systems. Health and safety, social justice, and environmental impact are at the top of the agenda for many workers and, likewise, for many employees, customers, shareholders and other stakeholders. And yet, at the same time, there is broad recognition that offices and workplaces are at the heart of organizational culture, creativity, and talent attraction – fundamental keys to individual and organizational success.

The opportunity to write a book about this pivotal moment was too compelling an opportunity to pass up. Across diverse cultures and societies, work and workplace are evolving through multiple dimensions. The best thing I did was to enlist my colleagues Ben Breslau and Peter Miscovich – both prolific thinkers, researchers, and writers in their own right. To no one's surprise, the response was an immediate and enthusiastic *yes*. Over many months, through holidays and long weekends, they juggled work, home, and family priorities, yet nonetheless were able to devote precious time to this endeavor.

Our understanding of what constitutes a workplace has been fundamentally redefined as it becomes increasingly clear that work is not a place you go to but something you do – a phrase you will encounter again.

In our daily work lives, we collaborate every day with organizations that are pioneering new approaches to their workplaces, buildings, and real estate portfolios. These owners, occupiers, and operators of corporate real estate represent a rich repository of experiences and knowledge that we have drawn from throughout the book. We were fortunate – and grateful – for the unanimous support we received from our clients so willing to share their workplace innovation stories.

In the pages ahead, we seek to navigate these combined experiences to provide a window into the probable and a glimpse into the possible – personal, responsible, and experiential workplace for the future of work. We hope you find the book thought-provoking and worthy of sparking debate. Most important, we trust you will uncover trends and ideas to inspire the future of work and workplace in your organization and in your personal lives.

Sanjay Rishi

# INTRODUCTION

A global software powerhouse, a bank that changed the very definition of innovation, and a technological and research leader with envied brand recognition in industries as diverse as defense, intelligence, and health care. Together, these three companies represent more than half a million employees and partners who have filed in and out of almost 100 million square feet of offices – the equivalent of five of the largest stadiums in the world – every day. These workplaces, and the work done within by the talented workers, have fueled lifestyles, successes, prosperity, security, and health around the world.

Workplaces have served as gathering spaces for generations of workers in pursuit of success, but, just as important, as places where people find fulfilment, a sense of belonging, and opportunities to learn and grow. In varying measures, organizations have used their workplaces and offices as sources of competitive advantage.

For these three companies, and many more in the following pages, workplaces are where brands are created, unique cultures are fostered and environments fashioned to inspire the contributions of the workforce. Their leaders view the workplace as foundational to business success and are willing to invest in creating welcoming, friendly spaces that, in turn, allow their people to prosper. These are just three stories to inspire as we look at the ways in which work is evolving and at the workplace we need now.

## Microsoft

More than a decade ago, Microsoft recognized changes in the way its products and services were developed and the need for the workplace to support a more agile and collaborative work style. New insights led to a substantial change in the company's office design, modernizing offices across the globe, while embarking on an ambitious 3-million-square-foot redevelopment project at its Redmond, Washington, headquarters that will shape the lives and work of its associates for decades to come.

The redevelopment now underway replaces legacy buildings primarily featuring closed offices with new team-based work-spaces supported by technology to enhance the work experience. Retaining only a small portion of the original Microsoft campus, the new design incorporates the needs of the workforce today, to address the way work is evolving. Collaboration and creativity will create a new, refreshed, energized experience at Microsoft, with workplaces designed to support smaller development and project teams.

The new spaces at Microsoft are designed to spark innovation and creativity, taking collaboration to new heights, leveraging digital capabilities to harmonize lives in and around work. No surprise, of course, that Microsoft is employing its extensive digital and cloud technologies acumen to make work and workplaces effective and easy to traverse, occupy, configure, and engage. Work-place apps will enable employees to reserve workspaces; personalize their workdays, work groups, and spaces; and seamlessly access transit and rideshare applications. Easy access to health and wellness data and amenities will afford employees time and resources for rejuvenation and recharging. Wayfinding tools will help guests and employees efficiently locate spaces and people for interactions. As the Microsoft ecosystem fuels the brain, apps will help employees fuel their bodies with easy access to food, exercise, yoga, and light-filled spaces.

Microsoft is using its own Microsoft Azure platform to manage a portion of the buildings at its headquarters campus and at locations around the world. Incorporating Azure Digital Twins technology, facility managers can digitally model physical space layers, with real-time data anonymization, to learn about the spaces people are using and how they are using them, informing data-driven space planning and allocation. The Azure platform also ensures that buildings operate efficiently to minimize energy and waste, and optimize indoor air quality.

## Capital One

You can't miss the towering presence of Capital One, a global brand that is considered a leader in innovation and banking, as you drive down the Washington, DC, beltway. The landmark campus attracts employees and the community to the promise and ambition of this bank that has embraced digital capabilities to differentiate itself, redefining brand and customer intimacy.

Live-work-play is coming together seamlessly in the Capital One headquarters, encompassing an amphitheater, a biergarten, hotel rooms, a 1,600-seat corporate events and performing arts center, retail, and workspaces that all flow fluidly to enable the next waves of innovation and growth. Easy access to the Metro, ample smart parking, and a design that embraces all modes of traveling to and within the campus, including footpaths and bicycle trails, makes access to and from the buildings efficient. Once again, experience is central to the significant capital investment, and the value of a differentiated workplace is clearly embraced in Capital One's goal of attracting and retaining top talent.

As guests arrive at Capital One's seventh-floor sky lobby, the experience is more akin to visiting a world-class hotel or restaurant than a leading bank. Each floor is connected with interior stairs, alternating on either side of the building, to make employees on each level feel connected. Open seating areas around each staircase allow for impromptu meetings. Art and sculptures line the walls and halls are strategically placed to inspire associates and create a sense of connectedness to surrounding communities.

## Leidos

A world leader in technology and research, Leidos stands apart in the complex industries it serves, which include defense, intelligence, and health care. One of the largest government contractors on the planet, Leidos manages complex challenges on a daily basis as it operates across the globe – and its workplaces mirror that complexity. Few organizations anywhere in the world have facilities that manufacture the next lunar lander, precision-guided munitions, under- and over-water combat vehicles, while also operating wet labs for cancer research and other facilities that produce and distribute vaccines – including those used to combat Ebola. Add to this diverse portfolio the highly regulated government and intelligence agency facilities where Leidos employees provide expertise.

Leidos's new headquarters opened just as the world was shutting down in 2020. The sparkling new facility in Reston, Virginia, was not vacant for long, however. Leidos's mission-critical work brought people into the office spaces designed to promote a sense of belonging, teaming, and energy. Digital technologies deployed across the offices allow seamless, touchless, productive connectivity and navigation across the airy, bright spaces.

What makes these organizations stand out is that their workplaces reflect their distinct brands. Their real estate portfolios are designed to add value by attracting and retaining scarce talent in a time of unprecedented demographic shifts. Their workplaces transcend the simple function of a place to work.

The undeniable reality in this postpandemic world is that workplaces as we know them are on the verge of unprecedented transformation. The pandemic shattered long-accepted individual, business, and societal norms, and unleashed uncertainty at an unforeseen pace and magnitude. Demographic shifts, health and safety, and digital disruption are among the drivers of these accelerating trends.

These three organizations are by no means exceptions of foresight, and the following pages unravel many such stories of innovation and differentiation. Enterprises large and small, public and private, are grappling today with challenges, as well as opportunities, shaping their pursuits of success. Industry sectors and communities are assessing cyclical versus structural shifts as the post-COVID-19 world takes shape. Corporate C-suites are adapting to new realities and uncertainties.

These trends have been clearly evident over the last few years. Never before in history, however, has the topic of workplace been top-of-mind for the C-suites and leaders of organizations. Likewise, never before have individuals challenged the nature of work.

The pandemic shall pass, as pandemics always do, but the learnings and experiences of a year-long world of virtual work will remain. The monumental change that organizations and their workforces had to endure also surfaced a number of questions that companies must now grapple with.

What are workplaces of tomorrow going to look like? Is a virtual work environment truly conducive to productivity, innovation, culture, and collaboration over the long term? How will organizations attract and retain talent in the future, and drive performance and culture for their people? How will work evolve? How must capital be deployed to harness the promise of tomorrow? What is the right balance of work from home and work from work? And, most important, how can we optimize our work, workforce, and workplace?

From a workforce perspective, personal desires, preferences, needs, and wants dominate employee desire to contribute to success today. Workers are asking themselves, "Where should I live? Where should I work? How do I work? When do I commute and how do I collaborate?" With the untethering of work from an official workspace, the individual is exercising the "I" at work.

The good news is that the next few years hold the very real promise of being judged by history as the inflection point of innovation and growth. Now is the launching point for a new approach to work, workforce, and workplace.

Harnessing today's and tomorrow's digital capabilities will unleash the creativity and ability of individuals and workgroups to tailor the way ideas proliferate and responsibilities are executed. The very real drive toward a better world is becoming manifest through multiple dimensions influencing workplace strategies. Sustainability and social responsibility deliver economic benefits, while also addressing the more altruistic goals of a healthier planet.

This book offers a comprehensive exploration of the workplace of today and its various influences. It provides a window into the probable and a glimpse into the possible. A personalized, responsible, experiential workplace emerges (see Figure I.1).

In the following pages, we have extensively explored the imperatives to change, provided experiences of organizations and individuals from across the world, and debated options and approaches to bringing these transformed workplaces to life. We evaluated perspectives of organizations that occupy offices, invest in workspaces, and employees who make up the workforce of today – diverse, individualistic, engaged, and competitive. Those perspectives coalesced on a distinct viewpoint: the workplace is the beating heart of an organization and will continue to be so; enterprises must pull the various levers

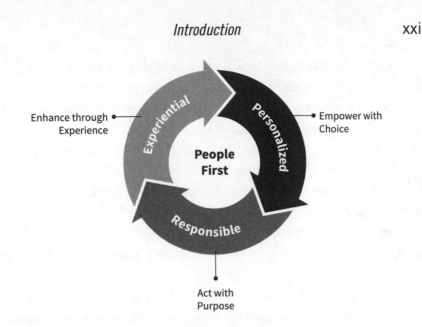

Enhance through
Experience

Empower with
Choice

**People
First**

Act with
Purpose

**Figure I.1   Future of Work: Workplace Framework**
**The workplace must provide memorable experiences;**
**a sense of purpose, belonging, and corporate responsibility;**
**and the power to personalize through the workplace.**

of workplace transformation to harness the power of their workforces; creating a culture of collaboration and a sense of belonging
is paramount to talent attraction, retention, and overall success of an
organization.

We bring to the book the blending of our combined career learnings – a total of more than 75 years – along with the deep expertise
of our extensive group of passionate collaborators. Our experiences
span careers in digital transformation, real estate strategy, enterprise
strategy, innovation, and research. Examples of approaches, thanks
to the collaboration of our clients cited across these pages, provide
illustrative vignettes to navigate these uncharted waters of the newly
emerged picture of workplace.

In Part I, we focus on the personal workplace. We start by exploring the imperatives that are changing the nature of workspaces and, in
turn, suggesting that organizations anticipate and develop a strategic

response to those imperatives. For the first time in history, four generations coexist in the workplace. Each generation brings with its own unique learnings, cultures, experiences, and expectations. Working collaboratively, these generations create value and success for their organizations. Yet, their preferences, allegiances, and portability across jobs and roles diverge significantly.

As much as multigenerational workers desire workplace flexibility and personalization, that flexibility is driven or limited by the availability of tools and technology. The speed of corresponding workplace evolution will be driven by the level of organizational commitment to change.

The responsible workplace, with its various dimensions, is emerging as the next major driver of change for organizations. Corporate responsibility now goes much farther than it did in the past, when it mostly comprised well-intentioned initiatives to further the corporate culture. Part II lays out the case for change and uncovers a mandate for organizations to invest financial, human, and social capital to effect fundamental change.

We define four macro responsibility imperatives: health and wellness, environment and sustainability, diversity/equity/inclusion, and resilience. Members of today's workforce are driving as they seek to blend working from the home, from the office, and from anywhere. They care about societal causes, including glaring problems of social and racial injustice, income inequality, and environmental sustainability. They want the workplace to support a distinct culture and opportunities for collaboration, creativity, and community, and they're relying on their employers to build such a space. The challenge, of course, is to address the divergent needs and preferences of workers themselves. We examine four worker profiles whose divergent needs are a source of challenge and opportunity.

In Part III, we explore the experiential workplace. Experience indeed is everything – in personal lives and in lives at work.

Individuals are motivated to come to work to find social interaction, mentorship, collaboration, and learning. Workplaces are evolving rapidly to accommodate these heightened needs of individuals. C-suite executives increasingly recognize that workplaces should be inviting and healthy, and facilitate a rewarding experience. Talent attraction and retention rests on this focus on workplaces that help create a brand and a sense of belonging that can be illusive in a digitally enabled world.

We unpack design influences that are affecting physical spaces. The innovation and creativity in the physical design shape the first visual experience for the visitor. Much can be leveraged from ideas and concepts that leading enterprises are creating and adopting. We further explore the intelligent experience – the coming together of the physical and the digital. In leading companies, digital transformation is enabling not only new business models but also new workplace experiences. Mobile apps are making navigation easy, space reservations efficient, occupancy management effective, and the entire spectrum of sustainable, responsive, smart workplace operations a reality.

Not unlike industries that have harnessed digital and cloud technologies to power innovation, workplaces stand to benefit from the enhanced postpandemic attention to the domain of corporate real estate. Commercial property technology – "proptech" – has been fueled by investments across the globe, and the pandemic has enabled a marked acceleration of a whole new spectrum of capabilities, including artificial intelligence (AI), machine learning, augmented and virtual reality, and touchless technologies, to name a few, into the workspace.

The dimensions of transformation are diverse, with no panacea or "one-size-fits-all" approach for organizations and workers to embrace. Yet, the trends, the needs, and the capabilities for transforming workplaces are undeniable and the opportunity vast. The call to action has never been louder and the foundation of support never stronger, for organizations to navigate their individual journeys through the labyrinth of options.

The workplace of the future is here and now, and the lines between where we live, work, and play have become blurred. The experiential workplace is now the new metric by which spaces are being evaluated, as organizations seek to optimize their use of space while fostering employee engagement and productivity through dynamic workplace strategies.

We conclude the book in Part IV having described the emerging demand, the paths to fulfilment of those demands, and the risks of inaction. Relying on the assessments and views of the entire ecosystem of workspace participants – investors, occupiers, brokers, managers, proptech entrepreneurs, corporate real estate officers, human resource leaders, chief information officers, and more – we aim to help organizations and individuals think through the continuum of needs and priorities across six facets of workplace transformation.

Since many of these issues and trends are still emerging, with no one "right answer" for the workplace, we have sought to provide a strategic framework whereby companies can discover the approach that will meet their unique corporate management, organizational, workforce, and cultural needs. The proposed framework is a tool for decision-making and capital investments that can be customized to each organization. It reflects approaches that leading organizations are adopting to fit their particular circumstances.

# PART

# I

# The Personalized Workplace

*"My philosophy is that everything starts with a great product."*
Steve Jobs, Co-Founder, Apple Inc.

Consider your favorite products and what you love about them. Is it the style? Maybe they are particularly practical or intuitive. Do they serve their purpose well? Do they provide great value?

They are probably easy to access and increasingly interoperable, or at least compatible, with other products you use. If they are innovative and entertaining, too, you may find it hard to live without them. And, depending on your shopping preferences, you may find they are made by companies committed to environmental sustainability, fair labor practices, and other public benefits.

Your favorite products likely engage you in a personal way by responding to your needs. They probably aren't custom-built for you, but rather *developed in a way that feels personalized* or configurable for your needs. Such products don't dictate when you use them, but instead draw you to them. They often offer the ultimate *flexibility* in how, when, and why you use them.

Think about your iPhone, your Peloton, your favorite pair of jeans, or even your favorite fancy latteccino made just the way you like it from your local coffee bar. When you feel like changing things up, you can consider additional options like a new mobile app, a different yoga or cardio workout, an of-the-moment accessory, or a passionfruit beverage from your friendly barista.

Now think about your workplace – that is, the one you frequented before the pandemic. Would you characterize it the same way you describe your personal items? Probably not. Yet, believe it or not, it's actually possible for a workplace to be all of those things – personalized, responsive, beneficial for public good, experiential. In fact, workplaces are going to have to become more like consumer products to meet the needs of workers now. For employers, now is the time to adapt the "product" – the workplace – for a personalized, responsible, and experiential future (see Figure I.1).

We live in a world of seemingly endless options and instant gratification. To stand apart, consumer brands have had to find ways to create emotional connections with their customers, almost instantly. Why should the workplace be any different?

People have more options than ever in where, how, and when they work, including more opportunities to work with companies located around the world, or even to start their own business as a freelancer or gig worker. Organizations must find ways to spur affinity, create community, and engage workers far beyond their daily tasks.

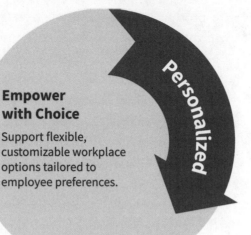

**Empower with Choice**

Support flexible, customizable workplace options tailored to employee preferences.

Personalized

**Figure I.1　The Personalized Workplace**
**The personalized workplace is responsive to**
**employee needs and preferences, and will empower talent**
**with a choice of workplaces and spaces.**

Like a product, the workplace must be designed, measured, and marketed. It must meet the essential needs of its customers – your workforce – and embody your brand promise and values. It must be continually optimized and proven effective, from both a space and social perspective. And, finally, it must draw in talent and keep them engaged and productive.

This isn't the workplace of the past, or even of one year ago. A new world of work is emerging. Are you confident you're creating the workplace you need now?

# 1 | The Origin and Evolution of Workplace

*"Those who cannot remember the past are condemned to repeat it."*
George Santayana, Philosopher

Today, most C-suite leaders recognize that great workplaces and workplace strategies can help win the war for talent and provide competitive advantage. That recognition is a relatively recent development, however. With a few notable exceptions, organizations historically have viewed the workplace as a location to get work done and a necessary expense. Today, a more sophisticated view of workplace is emerging.

To understand where we're headed, let's understand how we got here. The first dedicated corporate office buildings began to pop up in London in the early eighteenth century, housing the likes of the Royal Navy and the East India Trading Company. With the British Empire expanding and creating trading routes across its empire and the world, the concept of a centralized and dedicated physical space in which to administer a growing enterprise – and all its paperwork – began to take shape.[i]

In the United States, the corporate office dates back to the middle of the nineteenth century, when railroads expanded economic and geographic prospects. The complexity of growing businesses demanded a new physical workplace model.

Since that time, the workplace has evolved only incrementally through economic and business cycles, social and military crises, and industrial and technological revolutions.[ii] In the early to mid-twentieth century, offices were designed with efficiency in mind. Little attention was paid to the quality of the environment for employees. Using the efficiency strategies of mechanical engineer Frederick Taylor, many offices simply squeezed employees together to toil under the watchful eyes of supervisors, in an effort to boost productivity. Meanwhile, offices were growing bigger as advances in architecture, engineering, and construction led to larger buildings. Skyscrapers began to dot skylines of New York, Chicago, San Francisco, London, and other major cities around the world.

The 1960s saw a move away from the endless rows of workstations lined up to maximize space. Post-Taylorism, the concept of "office landscape," or *Bürolandschaft* as coined by a German design team, promoted the idea of breaking up rows of desks into smaller, organic cluster of workspaces with small privacy partitions. The goal was to create a less hierarchical workplace that fostered collaboration and socialization, not just productivity.

As buildings grew taller, space design grew more creative, too, allocating space for work, secretarial teams, meetings, and eating. *Bürolandschaft* eventually evolved into the concept of the "action office," the brainchild of Herman Miller's Robert Propst. Propst was among the first industrial designers to recognize that the workplace environment affects the ability to perform mental work. He conceived of the action office as an environment where workers would have the space and privacy to perform their work, instead of being elbow-to-elbow with coworkers. Ironically, what eventually emerged was the modern-day cubicle,[iii] with fabric-covered walls and modular flexibility – which evolved into ubiquitous and uninspiring "cube farm."

The widespread adoption of cubicles contributed to generic, albeit functional, office interiors at the same time the growing sophistication of consumer product branding began to influence corporate building exteriors. By the 1960s, companies like IBM were building unique headquarters designed to embody their brands. Completed in time for the 1972 Olympic Games, BMW's famed world headquarters building in Munich, Germany, resembles the four cylinders of a car engine. However, the brand concept was typically expressed only in the exterior architecture of these facilities, rather than in the experience of the workplaces inside.

By the 1980s, large corporations had mostly shifted once again toward a focus on productivity, with profitability as the primary motive, per economist Milton Friedman's mandate that the primary objective of business is to maximize returns to shareholders. In an era of junk bonds and leveraged buyouts, Wall Street investment banks became infamous for working their junior associates around the clock. Cubicles shrunk in size while their walls grew higher, isolating workers from everything but the task at hand.

With the focus on profitability and productivity, it's no wonder that the cubicle rose to prominence. The C-suite viewed workplace as a cost and utility with limited choice, not a creative, inspired, or desired product with a compelling value proposition for the employee-consumer. At most companies, regardless of industry, purpose, or workforce demographics, offices were homogenous and bland. Employee workplace enjoyment, comfort, and collaboration were not prioritized.

Office environments remained unimaginative through the end of the twentieth century. Layouts of desks and furniture were of varying generic styles and formats, with some private offices, a smattering of conference rooms and a vending machine, café, or other simple and fixed amenities situated under the glow of florescent lights.

The dot.com boom and bust sent the cubicle walls tumbling down. By the 2000s, young technology companies began pioneering creative offices designed to attract and retain the best and brightest in-demand talent. These companies quickly realized collaboration among these sought-after workers resulted in better ideas, faster innovation, and seamless information sharing. Cubicles gave way to open work areas and bench seating that fostered an open dialogue – and provided greater flexibility and higher-density space to accommodate rapid growth.

As their companies grew, Silicon Valley technology leaders looked beyond the office interior to design unique suburban campuses that attract and inspire talent, bringing their corporate mission and culture to life, often in spectacular fashion. Creative companies took the opportunity to incorporate fun and whimsy – sometimes to the extreme – through art and engaging installations like large aquariums, living walls of plants, or game rooms. Flexibility trumped privacy and focus, and, occasionally, practicality.

The sprawling "Googleplex" in Mountain View, California, headquarters of Google and its parent company Alphabet became a poster child for the new age of technology workplace. In 2015, Facebook hired then-86-year-old architect Frank Gehry to build its new "airplane hangar" headquarters in Menlo Park, California. In 2017, Apple upped the ante, delivering its futuristic Norman Foster-designed "spaceship" headquarters in Cupertino, California, at an estimated cost of $5 billion. Similarly, Microsoft's headquarters campus in Redmond, Washington, has continually evolved for 35 years and remains an iconic symbol of innovation.

These technology innovators were also workplace innovators, recognizing that the office was not just a place to work but an environment to spark creative thinking. Botanical gardens on rooftops and in courtyards, free premium and craft food options, and games and entertainment galore were designed to motivate talent to shape a unique culture.

Many amenities and perquisites introduced into the workplace had a well-intentioned purpose. On the frontlines of technology innovation, employees are expected to work long hours to meet aggressive product delivery deadlines. While technology companies weren't the first to recognize that providing live-work-play amenities could enable employees to be more productive, they raised the bar for workplace possibilities that made being on the frontlines of innovation more enjoyable.

Outside of the technology sector, other companies with unique brands and products have made similarly bold statements with their headquarters. Nike's world headquarters campus in Beaverton, Oregon, for example, embodies the company's mission to "bring inspiration and innovation to every athlete in the world" with buildings and fields named after many of the world's greatest athletes, along with sports performance centers and research labs where the company fuels its innovation. Similarly, Lego opened the first phase of its new corporate headquarters in Billund, Denmark, in late 2019 with the goal of creating a workplace that is playful and fun to inspire creativity. Lego bricks are incorporated into the building's exterior walls, and are referenced throughout the interior, from brightly colored staircases to Lego-created sculptures that adorn common areas.

In conjunction with the rise of the amenities-rich office emerged the idea that standard desks and chairs weren't the only path to productivity. Residential-style furnishings and activity-based workspaces for different kinds of work could also be highly beneficial. WeWork helped pioneer these concepts with its coworking spaces, complete with huddle booths, open spaces, benches, private offices, meeting rooms, and a comfortable design aesthetic.

Forward-looking companies began investing in humanized workplaces with creative layouts encompassing different kinds of workspaces and seating options. These new kinds of workplaces were intended to appeal to highly skilled and sought-after employees, while providing the right kinds of workspaces for collaboration, heads-down solo work, and private calls or meetings.

Only over the past decade has the idea of aligning the workplace with a company's mission and purpose spread beyond a select few brands. For some, the effort was more superficial or experimental than substantive, limited by cost pressures and financial performance concerns.

Nonetheless, these efforts formed the important prototypes of purposeful and experiential workplace environments that elevate the office above its roots as a place to get work done. The workplace has become part of the company brand and expression of its ethos, motivating the workforce to gather and achieve a common mission. The action office has evolved to the intelligent office, supporting multidimensional work, from deep concentration to customer engagement, "showroom" activities to extended reality experiential work.

As is usually the case, the future of the workplace had arrived – but even now, it hasn't been evenly distributed.

## The Value of Location

As workplaces have evolved – or should evolve – to more closely address the needs and preferences of employees, location has become part of the workplace strategy, too.

Over time, the location preferences for corporate offices have shifted, depending on the value equation, or the balance between the cost of real estate and the opportunities of a location in terms of the quality of the space, convenience, safety, and proximity to talent, customers, and jobs.

In the United States, for example, central business districts (CBDs) were the growing focus for decades as the centers of commerce and industry. Yet, many US urban areas lacked vibrancy and were perceived as challenged by crime and lack of cleanliness.

By 1960, the interstate system had opened the suburbs to urban workers, allowing them easy access to affordable and spacious housing, green space, and safety. Suburbia created a compelling value proposition for aspiring families throughout the 1970s and 1980s. Employers soon followed, establishing campus settings within easy drives to convenient suburban locations, often near highway interchanges.

The preference for the suburbs persisted until the 1990s and 2000s, when enterprising mayors and civic organizations revitalized urban areas with 24/7 amenities and a greater sense of safety. Cities once again became attractive to residents and employees, especially younger generations looking for a dynamic urban "vibe," cultural amenities, the convenience of public transportation, and a compact, high-density, live-work-play environment.

Employers were quick to follow employees back to the urban environment, as evidenced by the rush of corporate campus relocations and expansions in CBD and emerging urban locations during the past 20 years. Prime examples include Google's offices in Manhattan, GE's location in Boston, McDonald's downtown Chicago headquarters, and Amazon's facilities in Seattle and Washington, DC's near-suburb of Crystal City, Virginia. Urban areas became more dynamic and competitive, offering the best overall value for corporate employers seeking to attract the next generation of workers.

Now, the value equation is shifting again. Urban environments and big gateway cities have grown increasingly expensive, with housing costs rising more quickly than the wages of the average worker. In the pandemic environment, cities became less desirable – albeit perhaps temporarily – and the remote working option made it easier for employees to live and work far from their corporate homes.

Thanks to the combination of the natural aging of the giant millennial generation – creating new households and families – and the newfound flexibility of remote working, Sun Belt cities and suburban (or "outer urban") environments are seeing growing popularity, at least temporarily. Sun Belt and suburban markets outperformed traditional CBDs in terms of commercial real estate rents and occupancy during the pandemic. Many of these new "growth markets" enjoy demographic tailwinds and other advantages that make it likely that they will continue to prosper. But have no doubt, the great urban gateway cities will rise and prosper once again, filled with great companies and young talent. As evidenced by population shifts from cities to suburbs and back again, future changes are likely inevitable over time.

## Next-Generation Remote Working

Demographic shifts had already begun to affect workplaces well before the pandemic, with the idea of a seamless live, work, and play environment starting to take hold in varying measures. Technology companies had been praised for creating a completely different kind of workplace, with amenities, sports and fitness spaces, and collaboration spaces to attract and retain up-and-coming talent. Companies in other industries sought to adopt similar concepts, with the expectation that doing so would enable them to be equally talent-centric and driven by creativity.

However, the emergence of this new type of workplace was not without challenges. The novelty of amenities gave way to a realization that installing smoothie bars and collaboration zones was not enough to declare that a cultural shift had occurred. Early adopters outside the tech space realized that a foosball table without a broader workplace philosophy didn't really amount to much. The culture of organizations and regions, the preferences of individuals in various geographic locations around the country and the world, and the nature of the work itself were all cited as reasons to exchange a one-size-fits-all approach to workspaces no matter how amenities-heavy – with greater alignment to the ethos and culture of each organization.

And then came the pandemic, which brought upheaval in perceptions and experiences of individuals and organizations. The rapid movement of work from offices to homes demonstrated – at times surprisingly – the vast possibilities for productive workers contributing to organizational success from more diverse workplace settings. Some have suggested the possibility of all office work being performed remotely. While the debate rages on about the various dimensions that impact the question of why organizations need an office, the idea that workplaces will disappear entirely has been convincingly dismissed. The idea that workplaces will likely need to change and evolve is also an agreed-upon truth.

As the largest work-from-home experiment since the advent of the corporate office, our recent experiences have shown that remote work can be effective – although not everyone wants to work remotely all the time. Now, some C-suite leaders are questioning how productive their remote workers have really been, how much office space their companies actually need, and what the real purpose of that space should be.

It's important to remember that the pandemic era is not the first time that major companies have attempted remote work at scale. Previous remote-work initiatives during the 1970s through the 1990s taught many painful lessons on the shortcomings of large-scale work-from-home approaches, particularly at companies where culture was not well defined. In these experiments, organizations had at least some of the technology to accomplish large-scale remote work. Yet, many fell behind the progressive leaders that had continued to focus primarily on their physical offices as talent magnets and innovation centers. Early on, companies attempting the mixed-mode workplaces often unintentionally created an information disconnect between those in the office and remote workers, and fell behind in innovation and performance. Ultimately, some returned to requiring most employees to work in the office, whether all or at least some of the time.

Companies with sizable remote work programs were the exceptions. In advanced economies, only a small share of the workforce – typically 5–10 percent – regularly worked from home before the pandemic.[iv] Our comfort with remote work has improved by necessity and through advancements in connectivity, collaboration, and management technologies.

Companies across industries are now refining their remote work policies in response to employee expectations and the demands of their businesses. Many are likely to embrace increased workplace flexibility as a talent recruitment and retention strategy, and to open the door to working with the best talent regardless of location – an inevitable shift accelerated by the pandemic.

Some of the progressive companies leaning into the remote workplace are the very companies that provide enabling technology for remote working and virtual collaboration. Dropbox, for example, has shifted to a "virtual first" workplace, allowing employees to perform their individual work remotely and return to physical office hubs for collaboration and team-building purposes.

"Demand is coming back," says Andy Gloor, CEO of Sterling Bay, a leading owner/operator real estate investment and development company that *Crain's Chicago Business* calls "Tech industry's go-to real estate developer." Recent high-profile projects completed by Sterling Bay under Gloor's leadership include corporate headquarters for McDonald's and Google.

Gloor's clients are convinced that "culture, brand, and teamwork just don't work in a remote work environment," he says. While Gloor does agree that some job profiles may be appropriate for work from home, he sees the vast majority of his clients, leading corporations and global leaders amongst them, continuing to build their success and future with talent coalescing in the workplace. He also sees some clients that had densified their spaces to high degrees now have additional space requirements to allow for social distancing in the workplace.

Emerging from the pandemic, companies face new urgency to tackle the complex journey to the future of work. Forward-looking companies are creating hybrid workplace strategies that blend remote and on-site working and, ideally, boost employee performance by providing workspace choice. Also important, companies recognize that their workplace strategies won't necessarily be static. Always-on transformation will likely become the new imperative as employees embrace the idea that work is something you do, not a place you go – and sometimes the work you do is best done in the office setting.

In the future of work, many companies will pursue talent strategies based on geographically dispersed full-time employees and on-demand "liquid workforce" of people who may or may not ever set foot in the corporate office. "Talent anywhere" is now being considered as a legitimate component of corporate workforce strategy, looking beyond geographic borders to find the best employees who may be fully remote or in ecosystems of talent clusters in multiple dispersed locations.

Amidst a continuing global war for talent, employers will need to shape the workplace at least partially around the needs of employees, rather than vice versa. Health, wellbeing, work-life balance, corporate responsibility, and a sense of purpose have become more important than compensation alone as motivations for working and must be reflected in day-to-day work experience. Companies must determine how and where to provide the right kinds of workplace and workspace options for their unique talent networks.

Our research[v] shows that most companies plan to embrace a new hybrid workplace strategy, in which the office will remain central and critical in an ecosystem of workers and workplaces (see Figure 1.1). New strategies are essential to meeting employee expectations, with 79 percent of employees reporting that they want to be able to come into the office at least some of the time. Moving

**Figure 1.1   The Evolving Workplace Ecosystem**
**Hybrid working likely involves working in the corporate office**
**most of the time and working at home or elsewhere – a coffee**
**shop, an airport lounge, a coworking space, for example – at**
**other times.**

forward, the big question for companies and employees will be how to make the hybrid workplace enable, align, and empower teams to drive enterprise and employee value. Companies seeking to drive purpose and performance will need to focus on the principles of personalization, corporate responsibility, and a multidimensional workplace experience.

## SOURCES CITED

i. "History of Office Design," K2space, November 1, 2019, https://k2space. co.uk/knowledge/history-of-office-design/.

ii. Kaley Overstreet, "A Brief History of Workplace Design and Where It Might Be Headed Next," *Archdaily*, May 29, 2020, https://www.archdaily.com/940538/ a-brief-history-of-workplace-design-and-where-it-might-be-headed-next.

iii. Nikil Saval, "The Cubicle You Call Hell Was Designed to Set You Free," *Wired*, Conde Nast, April 23, 2014, https://www.wired.com/2014/04/how-offices-accidentally-became-hellish-cubicle-farms/.

iv. Susan Lund, Anu Madgavkar, James Manyija, and Sven Smit, "What's Next for Remote Work: An Analysis of 2,000 Tasks, 800 Jobs, and Nine Countries," McKinsey & Company, March 3, 2021, https://www.mckinsey.com/featured-insights/future-of-work/whats-next-for-remote-work-an-analysis-of-2000-tasks-800-jobs-and-nine-countries.

v. Flore Pradère, JLL Research, "Worker Preferences Barometer," JLL, May 2021, https://www.us.jll.com/content/dam/jll-com/documents/pdf/research/ global/jll-global-worker-preferences-barometer-may-2021-updated.pdf.

# 2 | Personalizing the Workplace

*"If you want to create a great product, just focus on one person. Make that one person have the most amazing experience ever."*

Brian Chesky, CEO, Airbnb

During the past decade or so, leading companies have begun to view their workplace as a consumer product – that is, a service or resource that employees can consume just as they might "consume" a residence, a hotel room, a cell phone, or a new car. Many of the products we consume these days can be personalized and configured with a single swipe or tap, but the workplace – whether physical or digital – has historically been less responsive, lacking the kind of personalization that individuals might expect or desire.

Yet, if the workplace could be consumed in a more personalized way, it would unleash significant improvements in engagement, performance, and value. Consider the simple office layout. The working world is filled with analysts and administrative assistants who struggle to be productive in one-size-fits-all open-plan environments. If provided with some level of privacy and a quiet workspace, and perhaps the flexibility to work quietly at home, these beleaguered workers could become top performers. The office may provide space – but is it the right kind of space for different kinds of work?

Conversely, thousands of lawyers, managing directors, and executives across industries thrive when they are closely connected to their employees and spending more time in collaborative environments. Yet, they are too often confined to enclosed offices that discourage interaction and encourage the type of heads-down work that no longer dominates their days at the office.

To be effective, the workplace must offer individual choice and control, with places to create the best experience and performance possible. Ideally, workplace strategy is a win-win: companies need workplaces that achieve company objectives and are aligned with their mission and values, while employees need workplaces that are mapped to preferences for location, communication, automation, and design. Also important, organizations need workplaces that adapt to how the business is evolving and how you and your teams work most effectively, with data and predictive tools to guide workplace modifications that boost engagement, performance, health, and fulfillment.

What could that look like? Imagine coming to the office on a typical day. A workplace mobile app helps you find a parking spot or see when the next shuttle arrives to transport you from your transit station to the office. Making your way, you use the mobile app to reserve several workspaces for the day – a private telephone room for calls, an unassigned desk for checking emails, and a meeting space. The office is filled with natural light, plants, color, and art that conveys the energy and spirit of the corporate brand.

On the way to your first workspace of the day, a chance encounter with a colleague leads to an impromptu huddle in a convenient casual seating area with an interactive whiteboard. Afterward, you settle down into your private room to make some calls – after adjusting the lights and temperature to your preferred levels. A few hours later, the mobile app notifies you that it's time for a break, so you take a quick stroll through a Zen garden and then use your app to order a healthy lunch. You leave energized and fulfilled, rather than frustrated and exhausted.

## The People-Centric Workplace

Great products are designed and built to solve human needs. Where the future of work is concerned, creating a people-centric workplace product begins with understanding the different kinds of employees and jobs that need workspaces. What do you know about your employees and their preferences?

One starting point for personalization is to understand where individuals fit into the continuum from rigid to flexible in terms of openness to varying workplace environments. As illustrated here, JLL's March 2021 global survey[i] of 3,000 employees revealed four primary worker profiles. Representing the far points of the spectrum are the traditional office worker and the free spirit. The former prefers to head to the office every day and the latter wants to avoid any commute to work and likes a variety of spaces. In between are varying preferences and personas, from the "experience lover" to the "wellness addict" (see Figure 2.1.)

Interestingly, our research[ii] shows that the two extreme profiles, traditional office workers and free spirit, are less engaged and fulfilled than the average employee and don't expect as much from their employer. Yet those in the middle, the experience lover and wellness addict, expect a lot from their employer in terms of experience and comfort. In short, four representative segments of workers, each with its own likes and dislikes, and in many variations will shape workplace planning for the foreseeable future.

**Figure 2.1  Worker Profiles**
A March 2021 JLL study of 3,000 workers around the world reveals four primary types of workplace participants, from traditional office worker to the free spirit. The two intermediate profiles – the experience lover and the wellness addict – have extremely high expectations in terms of comfort and human experience. Different organizations, industries, and regions tend to attract different worker profiles, and employees may share characteristics of more than one persona.

Understanding these potential worker profiles is important for building a successful workplace strategy. Part of being a resilient organization requires recognizing the needs of the workforce and then developing policies and procedures that cater to those needs, giving workers what they need to perform at their best no matter what situation may emerge.

Profiles vary by geographic region. Our research has shown that different organizations tend to attract different worker profiles, and some profiles are more prevalent in some regions because of culture and customs.

In France, Germany, and Japan, for example, the office remains a central place for employees to work in, likely because of a more conservative approach to management. Workers over age 50 – and public-sector employees, in particular – value an office workspace. Among office workers in India, the collegial, social aspect of the office is important, as well as the productive environment, according to our research.[iii]

For some workers, the driver is a lack of space or privacy at home, while, for others, there is status associated with an office job. Among Asia-Pacific major cities, high housing costs, multigenerational households, and small dwellings hamper productivity at home – but flexibility also matters.[iv] In Hong Kong, the average size of an apartment is 40 square meters (430.5 square feet), or about the size of three typical car parking bays in the city and 90 square meters in Singapore. Both economic powerhouses have among the smallest dwellings in the world.

Work-from-home plans are all the buzz elsewhere in the world, but in Hong Kong and Singapore, such arrangements may not gain traction with majority of the workforce because space constraints hamper productivity. A strong demographic aspect of Asian countries is their younger population. While young people may be more tech savvy, the office is an outlet for some to get away from parents and to socialize. Some just want to escape the multigenerational house. The quality of the work environment is a particular attractor for young people in India – nice campus, safe and clean environment, cheap food, free and reliable Wi-Fi, and lots of other young people.

In contrast, working from home is more popular with Canadian employees. Among industries, working from home has above-average popularity in the technology sector, where workers were already experimenting with remote work before the pandemic. Working from home is also attractive to many workers in traditional industries, such as heavy machinery, consumer products, banking, and insurance, where working from home some portion of the week is a desirable option.

Younger workers, on the other hand, frequently enjoy the option to occasionally work neither at home nor an office, but in a third-party space such as a co-working site or coffee shop. Gen Y, comprising 25- to 34-year-olds, isn't the only generation that appreciates flexible spaces. Among many workers, regardless of age or industry, the option to conduct business wherever they prefer is especially attractive.

Understanding what your target workplace "customers" need requires a thoughtful combination of ethnographic research and observation. Starting with a blank slate, rather than envisioning the end product, can help you understand the entire context in which your workplace "product" will be operating. As always, the simpler the solution, the better.

With human experience at the core, effective consumer product development is based on the fundamental belief that, if you truly understand the customer, provide an amazing user experience, and solve the right problem, you will generate demand for your product and see the performance results.

For example, by analyzing real-time data about your office occupancy, you might learn that every conference room is constantly booked, yet not fully occupied – suggesting that more, smaller meeting rooms would better suit real-life needs. Or, perhaps a particular 10-seat conference room is never booked, creating wasted space. By understanding why the room is never used, you can either make the room more appealing or repurpose the space for critical needs.

New product development – especially for digital products – is always iterative. An agile approach, fine-tuning to continually meet evolving customer needs, is likely necessary for sustained success. The workplace product itself, and the product development and management process for workplaces, should be fluid. Rather than fully designing, constructing, and branding a new workplace concept and aiming to "sell" it to employees, savvy companies have begun prototyping new concepts in order to test, adjust, test, adjust, and test and adjust again.

With all this talk of personalization, most leaders nonetheless understand that the workplace should match the vision, strategy, and operating framework of the company. An organization can't offer employees a "choose-your-own-adventure" workplace and still maintain the cohesion and culture needed to bring people together, solve complex problems, and innovate to win in an increasingly competitive market. However, companies can – and many are – becoming increasingly strategic in mapping workplace design to employee needs to attract, retain, and effectively harness top talent.

"We are an entrepreneurial, data-driven, test and learn company," Stefanie (Stef) Spurlin of Capital One says. "So, all of that has influenced how we have approached workplace design as we renovate or bring our spaces online. The hybridization of the workplace, and the extension of the workplace to allow work everywhere, is "really an expansion of our option set. We've got all these different options within the workplace. Home becomes just another option of that, an extension of your optionality and your choice based on the kind of work that you need to do."

An important foundational step is to really understand the workforce of today. While recent experiences unleashed a barrage of employee surveys of all shapes and sizes to gauge productivity, engagement, and wellbeing, it's equally important to gauge employee preferences when they are not in crisis. Ongoing personalization of the workplace requires a steady finger on the pulse of the organization, whether through employee surveys, focus groups, or tracking usage of office spaces.

## "Demographics Is Destiny"

Whatever methods are used to monitor and manage employees' workplace preferences, the results are likely to vary widely across demographic groups. As nineteenth-century French sociologist and philosopher Auguste Comte wrote, "Demographics is destiny." His point was that the unique characteristics and movements of the population are often slow to change and imperceptible in daily life compared to the latest high-frequency financial or economic event. Yet, demographic shifts typically have profound effects.

Today, the workforce is increasingly demographically diverse, multigenerational, digitally native, liquid, and distributed geographically. The workforce is changing in important ways, and it's getting more difficult to keep good talent. According to the January 2020 biannual Employee Tenure Summary,[v] the median employee tenure in the US was 4.1 years, but only 2.8 years for workers of ages 25–34 years. Younger workers are more likely to change jobs frequently, making them difficult to retain.

The liberation of some jobs and employees to work from anywhere postpandemic may increase this churn in the future, as location-agnostic job opportunities reduce some of the friction that once limited employees from moving on to new roles. How will your workplace ecosystem help to attract, engage, teach, and retain the multigenerational and diverse workforce needed to adapt and thrive into the future?

A big challenge today is the integration of several generations of workers, each with their own preferences and needs with respect to the workplace and relationships with others. Baby boomers are nearing retirement. Gen Xers currently occupy a good percentage of management roles, but millennials are quickly moving into those. Gen Zers, who have recently entered the workforce, often have very different attitudes and preferences when it comes to work, and techno-reliant Gen Alpha will be entering the world of work in the near future, upending the balance among generations once gain.

Millennials became the largest generation in the workforce in 2018, accounting for 35 percent of all workers according to US Census data.[vi] Gen Z is not far behind. Yet the differences between these two "young talent generations" are just as stark as those of the boomers and Gen Xers who continue to make up an essential part of the workforce. It often escapes us, but the oldest millennials turn 40 in 2021. They are at the table making decisions, driving product roadmaps, strategizing on mergers and acquisitions, and fueling growth in very fundamental ways. They are married, have school-aged children, and expect their workplaces to allow them their desired level of flexibility. In stark contrast to the early months of the pandemic, millennials don't relish working from home as much as they once did.

## Baby Boomers

Although youth has been the undeniable focus of organizations recently, in terms of talent search and workplace positioning, the dominant demographic trend in the developed world is not youth but aging people. Baby boomers number more than 70 million people, ranging in age from the late 50s to mid-70s and shaped by some combination of post–WWII optimism, the Cold War, and the sociopolitical activism of the 1960s. Despite the fact that approximately 10,000 baby boomers are retiring every day, 25 percent of the US workforce will be 55 or older by 2029 – a 12 percent increase over 2019, according to Bureau of Labor Statistics projections.[vii] Since 2000, the employment of people aged 65 and older in the United States has increased by 51 percent, while the total employment of people between 25 and 65 has actually fallen by 3 percent, a phenomenon *The Economist*[viii] dubbed "work until you drop."

This trend is due partly to the size of the baby boomer generation and partly to the fact that people are living and working longer, either by desire or necessity. While baby boomers may hold a more traditional view of the workplace informed by their career experience, many have been able to work effectively remotely during the pandemic. They are more likely to have space at home for an office and, given their comparably long track records, are also generally more stable and established in their careers. Baby boomers may also be more flexible locationally, given that they frequently have lower mortgage debt and less dependence on schools than younger generations, and need different amenities as they age and consider alternative working arrangements.

Older workers who are expecting to live longer, given advancements in medicine, may also need to work longer to support their retirements. In 1970, life expectancy for people who reached age 65 was 78 for men and 82 for women. Today, men and women who've reached 65 will on average live to ages 84 and 86, respectively. Of course, physical fatigue and mental stress are also risks if the work or workplace are not conducive to this age group, according to Harvard Health.[ix]

The work of tomorrow may not fit all the employees of the past or present, and reskilling and reverse mentoring will be needed. "New" professional careers later in life are a possibility for many, and instead of baby boomers catering to millennial talent, as was the case over the past 10–15 years, millennial and Gen Z leaders will need to find, employ, and manage boomers to fill key labor needs.

Your workplace has tremendous opportunity to offer accessible, intuitive, and inviting physical and digital workplace environments to tap into this multigenerational workforce. While many companies have been focused on building out open-plan offices and game rooms for younger workers, it's important to realize that the growing contingent of baby boomer workers places higher value on things like personal space, suburban office options, flexible scheduling, and very different amenities like tech support services and, increasingly, on-site health clinics.

They're also not content to just fade into the distance, given the rise of the "silver economy" of people over age 50 who want to continue working, even on a part-time or occasional basis. With

750 million seniors in the world as of 2021 and numbers rising, this cohort will certainly have an impact on the future of work. Senior workers are choosing to remain in the workforce longer than their predecessors, creating new challenges and opportunities for employers and commercial property owners who may need to make adjustments to help them continue to work.

## Gen X

In the United States, Generation X consists of about 65 million people who were born between 1965 and 1980. This generation is considerably smaller than the ones on either side and will create a demographic deficit of executive-age workers in the next decade as baby boomers retire. However, the cohort still comprises the second-largest current share of the US workforce, just behind millennials. Gen X members entered the workforce with wider expectations of higher education for employment and with a higher share of women working than the previous generation.

Gen X was at the forefront of the switch from analog to digital modes in their formative years, witnessing the advent of desktop computers, cell phones, and internet connectivity. As a result, they are highly adaptable and open to learning new technologies, as well as very collaborative and open to change. Known for independence and adaptability, Gen Xers care about work-life balance just as their successors the millennials do; they work well in flexible environments and value diversity, creative thinking, and fun at work.

## Millennials

Many organizations have been fixated on millennials (Gen Y), who comprise more than a third of the workforce as of 2020. Half of the members of this generation are still establishing themselves and trying to earn early career and financial success, while the other half is in or approaching the stage of their lives where they are progressing their careers, starting families, buying houses, and "adulting." They were molded by the careful nurturing and protection of their parents, the baby boomers, and also by growing up during the rise of the internet, the iPhone, and social media.

Their formative years included several once-in-a-lifetime crises, such as the global financial crisis and the COVID-19 pandemic. US millennials have significant student debt and lower home ownership rates than previous generations. Around the globe, this generation has postponed forming families, instead prioritizing education, careers, and leisure.

They have been painted with a broad brush of lofty expectations and a desire to change the world, but are perceived as having less "grit and grind" than previous generations.

Millennials have also become a powerful consumer group, with their spending power continuing to rise beyond that of Gen X, according to analysis by *Financial Times*.[x] Research suggests they may have less brand loyalty than previous generations, but are moved by company purpose; 83 percent consider it important for the companies they buy from to align with their values. The same is true for their employers, and the workplace is a prime environment for reinforcing purpose and values to resonate with this cohort. Conscious, local, and healthy lifestyles and workstyles have become as important for many millennial employees as finding a sense of purpose in their work.

Millennials are leading the drive for workplace experiences that also speak to corporate values. Far from feeling entitled to work in a "cool" space, millennials want to draw inspiration from their work environment in much the same way artists travel to new destinations for a spark of creativity. They crave fresh air, outdoor space, and natural materials, as well as a commitment to sustainability goals. With a front-row seat to the effects of climate change, millennials and their younger counterparts in Gen Z are eager to use their clout to champion sustainability and expect this dedication to carry into their work environment, from banning single-use plastics to sourcing sustainable office furniture.

## Gen Z

Following Generation Y, a.k.a. millennials, is Generation Z, which is almost as big, at 67 million in the United States. Globally, Gen Z is estimated to already be the largest generation, with 2.5 billion people and accounting for over 30 percent of the population, according to United Nations data.[xi] The leading edge of Gen Z, born in 1995, has started entering the workforce. These are 20-something workers you will be recruiting and catering to within the term of your next lease.

What's important to note is that their characteristics are a bit different than millennials. Compared to millennials at the same age, Gen Zers tend to be more risk-averse and more focused on safety and security. They drink less alcohol, are less likely to work during high school, have fewer intimate relationships, and have fewer independent experiences – they're more likely to have parents present during social engagements. The approaches that employers have adopted toward improving employee experience for millennials may need to change again.

In an annual report on work trends,[xii] Microsoft noted that Gen Z is the generation likely to be most affected by the pandemic, much as millennials were hit hard by the financial crisis. They have less experience to call on and fewer strong social ties to fall back on. Given the challenges with learning, networking, and gaining valuable experience in a remote workplace, it's perhaps not surprising that 8 percent more Gen Z workers than those of other generations reported difficulty in finding an appropriate work-life balance, saying they are under pressure, often feel exhausted after a typical work day, and crave advanced learning and development programs in the workplace.

This struggle hurts not only Gen Z but also the companies that employ them. Younger generations are essential to evolving businesses for the future, offering new ideas and challenging the status quo in ways more established workers seldom do. If Gen Z continues to feel disengaged and unable to bring in new ideas or even speak up during the meeting, companies will lose out on their critical perspectives.

Workplaces will have to offer experiential and social hubs within a physical work environment, as well as digital solutions, to get this generation fully immersed in work. For a generation that has grown up gaming, coding, and living in an omni-channel, often digital-first world, apps and experiential technology are no-brainers.

More traditional engagement methods for building social capital are also needed, with a focus on truly embracing authenticity. Gen Z is the most diverse generation in the United States yet,[xiii] with nearly half identifying as racial or ethnic minorities. They also care about societal causes, including racial, income, and environmental inequity. Are the workplaces ready to welcome and enact the changes necessary to address these glaring problems?

## Gen Alpha

Following Gen Z is Gen Alpha, who have not yet entered the workforce. Born between 2010 and 2025, the oldest members of this generation may start to work on a part-time basis in the next few years, while others will only be in their infancy. They, too, will shape the workplace, likely in ways we won't be able to imagine or predict.

So far, what we know about this generation is that they are more diverse and more digitally reliant and technologically adept than any prior generation. These workers will likely have a significant advantage in their familiarity with and reliance on the latest technology and they will expect their employers to make it readily available to them.

## Young Talent Adapting to Remote Work

Despite being tech savvy "digital natives" and less traditional in their approach to work, younger generations of talent report productivity challenges and frustration from working virtually during the pandemic, according to Microsoft's annual research on work trends. Millennials and Gen Z workers tend to have less space for home offices than more established Gen X or baby boomers, need collaboration and help from managers to learn and develop their careers, and may have more distractions at home from either roommates, young families, or in many instances, their parents.[xiv]

Millennials also frequently expect both partners to be active participants in raising children, in contrast to many current company leaders who often have much more traditional home lives and expectations about the separation of work and family time. These expectations have raised important questions about how cultural work norms may change to allow young mothers and fathers to play the role they want to at home and at work and how the workplace of the future may help with that desired balance. Young parents living with children are feeling the most "overwhelmed, under pressure, disenchanted, and worried about their jobs," according to JLL's March 2021 *Workforce Preferences Barometer*.

Young mothers have been particularly affected recently, with labor force participation for this category falling by 2.8 percent since November 2019.[xv] That's more than the total labor force reduction during the Great Recession. The number of women in the workforce today is the lowest since the 1980s! Yet 60 percent of graduating college students are female — something has to give. Will child care facilities be a more important component of office and workplace offerings in the future?

While the 2020 Zoom-a-thon and Microsoft Teams separated colleagues physically, video actually brought many workers unexpected glimpses into colleagues' personal lives. They were able to see colleagues' home offices, meeting their children or pets in unexpected intrusions, colleagues shared those unexpected moments where home life and work life come together. These intimate glimpses point to a different type of "personalization" that will likely be evident in the future human-centric office.

## Microsoft Leads with Digital

Michael Ford is corporate vice president of Microsoft's Global Real Estate and Security organization, which is no small task with a presence in 117 countries and a portfolio of approximately 38 million square feet. Ford leads a global team that delivers and operates global workplaces that are connected, accessible, sustainable, and secure for the best employee experience. To create that experience at Microsoft, Ford and his team are bringing together the physical workplace elements with the digital to enable Microsoft's corporate culture and innovation.

"Lead with digital," Ford says. Digital can help right away to respond to the fast-changing dynamics and employee productivity needs of the workplace. Ford considers the entire employee journey "from when employees leave home, commute to work, arrive, move across the campus, perform work, and return back home." As one would expect, Microsoft has deployed a comprehensive app and on-site productivity technologies to enable this experience. Shuttle and commute services, workspace, and conference room reservations, and access to dining and other amenities allow employees to optimize their time. Ford speculated that without these tools in place to streamline the campus experience, employees could be overwhelmed by daily tasks and unable to bring their most creative self into actual meetings.

Creating the best workplace experience requires more than just digital tools, however. "You must transform your space" as well. While digital enablement goes a long way, physical space transformation is critical and the company is actively updating its Microsoft headquarters and many of its global campuses.

"Not only are we creating productive work experiences for today's employees, but we are also building spaces for future employees – today's 8th grader," Ford says.

Microsoft conducted a study of youth ages 12–21 to better understand their expectations and preferences of the workplace and help inform the future design of its workspaces. More recently, Microsoft published its Work Trend Index, revealing urgent trends leaders should consider as hybrid work unfolds.

Across these updates, Microsoft is turning the traditional open-plan office design on its head. Leveraging research into how its engineers develop products and services, the resultant model is a "neighborhood" approach to design the company calls "Team-Based Spaces." Each company is unique in the way they work, but for a Microsoft team, "8 to 12 people is the sweet spot. We are designing these team spaces with a variety of support spaces such as focus rooms, where four or five people can assemble, conference rooms where up to 12 people can collaborate, phone rooms for privacy, and concentration zones where one or two people can innovate together. People want to collaborate with each other and hear important conversations that apply to their project. Our product release processes are faster when there is knowledge sharing."

With more employees and businesses embracing the new hybrid workplace model, Microsoft is committed to the value of bringing people together in the workplace. Ford is committed to delivering spaces that anticipate the different ways teams need to work together in this new environment while providing the flexibility and agility employees now require. A principle that Microsoft standardizes across its global work sites is inclusive design. Whether employees are working from home, at the workplace, or utilizing many of the unique team collaboration spaces, this philosophy is aimed at creating a sense of belonging and helping teams stay connected however they choose to work.

## The Liquid Workforce

The typical workplace tends to cater to the traditional employee in a traditional employer–employee longer-term relationship. However, the future of work is likely to be exponentially more "liquid." MIT Sloan has identified today's workforce as an ecosystem, "a structure that consists of interdependent actors, from within the organization and beyond, working to pursue both individual and collective goals," that will dominate the future of work.[xvi] An estimated one in four employees, totaling close to 40 million people in the United States, participated in some freelance, contract, or other nontraditional "gig work," either as a primary or supplemental capacity in 2020, generating 5.7 percent of the US GDP; that's $1.21 trillion in revenue to the United States – and gig work is a global phenomenon.[xvii]

While the level of side work dipped slightly in 2020 because of overall declining employment, the pandemic will inevitably be an accelerator for independent work. By 2025, MBO Partners expects that 54 percent of the US workforce will have engaged in some form of independent work in their careers. These independent and flexible work arrangements will increasingly appeal across generations, as baby boomers can extend their work opportunities part-time and with some flexibility and younger, more entrepreneurial generations can generate additional income, or build a career founded on independence, freedom, and variety of opportunity.

For employers, tapping the growing gig economy will provide a critical variability in labor and resource capacity, capabilities and cost, and the ability to access unique skills from anywhere they reside. Employers and managers now need to view their workforces in terms of both employees and nonemployees, which presents a challenge to creating a cohesive and integrated workplace ecosystem.

The workplace will need to engage, connect, and create experiences for workers of all types. Toward that end, you'll need to consider ways to leverage the physical and digital workplace ecosystem to connect contract workers to employees and to the company's mission and values. Think through the technology, scalability, and security implications of a growing contract workforce.

## The Bottom Line for the Personalized Workplace

Workplaces have historically been designed to be generic, created either for no one in particular or for one specific employee cohort at a specific time. Now it is clear that the workforce is increasingly diverse in terms of age, culture, skill set, experience, needs, and preferences. The workplace must be able to accommodate such variability and the broad range of individual needs. The workplace has to make all employees feel comfortable, energized, and aligned, while still being efficient overall and not overly customized.

The best businesses and workplaces remain people-centric. Employee morale, collaboration, and innovation are underappreciated and underweighted in the discussions around productivity and optimization. As a result, the low-hanging fruit often includes efforts to cut real estate expenses without regard for the broader impact on an organization.

Real estate is often one of the CFO's targets for savings. But the reality is that the cost and value of talent typically far exceeds the cost of real estate. Small changes in real estate costs are not likely to have a big impact on bottom-line results, especially in industries – including life sciences or technology – in which top talent commands high wages.

Many companies may find easy gains to be made by tightening and aligning office space and real estate portfolios to the new future of work. In addition to looking at real estate as a cost to be managed, companies should view the workplace as an opportunity to attract and retain a diverse group of the best and brightest – and create personalized environments and experiences to drive individual and business performance.

## SOURCES CITED

i.   "Workforce Barometer," JLL, March 2021.

ii.  Flore Pradère, "Shaping Human Experience," JLL, January 2021, https://www.us.jll.com/en/trends-and-insights/research/global-hybrid-work-models-emerging-worker-profiles.

iii. Flore Pradère, "From Productivity to Human Performance," JLL, October 2020, https://www.us.jll.com/content/dam/jll-com/documents/pdf/research/emea/uk/jll-uk-from-productivity-to-human-performance.pdf.

iv.  Gonzalo Portellano, "The A-Z of Future Workplace Design," JLL, November 11, 2020, https://www.jll.com.sg/content/dam/jll-com/documents/pdf/research/apac/ap/jll-the-a-z-of-future-workplace-design.pdf.

v.   "Employee Tenure Summary," US Bureau of Labor Statistics, US Bureau of Labor Statistics, September 22, 2020, https://www.bls.gov/news.release/tenure.nr0.htm.

vi.  Drew Desilver, "10 Facts about American Workers," *Pew Research Center,* August 29, 2019, https://www.pewresearch.org/fact-tank/2019/08/29/facts-about-american-workers/.

vii. "Projections Overview and Highlights, 2019–29: Monthly Labor Review," US Bureau of Labor Statistics, September 1, 2020, https://www.bls.gov/opub/mlr/2020/article/projections-overview-and-highlights-2019-29.htm.

viii. Buttonwood, "Work Until You Drop," *The Economist,* October 11, 2014, https://www.economist.com/finance-and-economics/2014/10/11/work-until-you-drop.

ix. "Working Later in Life Can Pay off in More than Just Income," Harvard Health, Harvard Health Publishing, June 2018, https://www.health.harvard.edu/staying-healthy/working-later-in-life-can-pay-off-in-more-than-just-income.

x. "Millennial Moment: How Millennials Become the World's Most Powerful Consumers," *Financial Times,* June 5, 2018, https://www.ft.com/millennial-moment.

xi. Lee Miller and Wei Lu, "Gen Z Is Set to Outnumber Millennials Within a Year," Bloomberg, August 20, 2018, https://www.bloomberg.com/news/articles/2018-08-20/gen-z-to-outnumber-millennials-within-a-year-demographic-trends.

xii. "2021 Work Trend Index: Annual Report," Microsoft, March 22, 2021, https://ms-worklab.azureedge.net/files/reports/hybridWork/pdf/2021_Microsoft_WTI_Report_March.pdf.

xiii. "Nearly Half of Post-Millennials Are Racial or Ethnic Minorities," Pew Research Center's Social & Demographic Trends Project, Pew Research Center, November 13, 2018, https://www.pewresearch.org/social-trends/2018/11/15/early-benchmarks-show-post-millennials-on-track-to-be-most-diverse-best-educated-generation-yet/psdt-11-15-18_postmillennials-00-00/.

xiv. "Why the Pandemic Is Forcing Millennials to Move Back Home with Their Parents," PBS, Public Broadcasting Service, December 1, 2020, https://www.pbs.org/newshour/show/why-the-pandemic-is-forcing-millennials-to-move-back-home-with-their-parents.

xv. "Pandemic Pushes Mothers of Young Children out of the Labor Force," Federal Reserve Bank of Minneapolis, Minneapolis Fed, February 2, 2021, https://www.minneapolisfed.org/article/2021/pandemic-pushes-mothers-of-young-children-out-of-the-labor-force#_ftn1.

xvi. Elizabeth J. Altman, David Kiron, Jeff Schwartz, and Robin Jones, "The Future of Work Is Through Workforce Ecosystems," MIT Sloan Management Review, January 14, 2021, https://sloanreview.mit.edu/article/the-future-of-work-is-through-workforce-ecosystems/.

xvii. "State of Independence," MBO Partners, April 1, 2021, https://www.mbopartners.com/state-of-independence.

# 3

## The Future Is Flexible

*"As hybrid work emerges as the preferred way of working, businesses need to reinvent themselves with the workforce being 'front of mind.' In the future of work that is increasingly worker-centric, the human experience will take center stage."*

*Christian Ulbrich, CEO and President, JLL*

Corporate America has been on a 40-year workplace optimization journey that was accelerated by the pandemic and has led to what we're now calling the hybrid workplace. The hybrid workplace assumes that work can happen anywhere, across a range of physical and digital spaces including, but not confined to, the office.

Workers want the ability, or flexibility, to work where, when, and how they choose. They want to have more control of their schedules and routines, as well as their workspaces. Although such a demand might have been viewed as fanciful or ludicrous a few years ago, this type of work flexibility is now a legitimate option. If nothing else, the pandemic made clear that knowledge work can also be completed outside the central workplace setting, just as it can be completed in different hours than the traditional 8:00 a.m. and 5:00 p.m., Monday through Friday. No wonder 88 percent of employees globally would like some flexibility in working hours and schedule.[i]

A majority of workers now prefer remote work for at least part of the work week. Our human experience research shows that 63 percent of employees across industries globally now desire the flexibility to continue to work remotely at least some of the time and wish to work away from the office 2.1 days per week postpandemic.[ii] Of the 2.1 days away from the office, 1.5 days will be spent at home and another half day, on average, from a third place like a hotel, café, client site, or coworking space. The realization that at least some work can be done productively from anywhere has been a welcomed liberation from the desk-job mentality of most office workers.

Yet, 79 percent of employees say they do still want to be able to come into an office, but perhaps not 100 percent of the time. According to our research, only 26 percent of workers want to return to the office full time, spending five days a week and eight-plus hours a day at a desk in an office. For the right role, they shouldn't have to, after demonstrating they can work remotely effectively and productively when supported by the right technology. For example, 100 percent of call center employees could potentially work from home permanently, while less than 10 percent of creative knowledge workers could successfully do so. It's also worth noting that many employees had this degree of flexibility before the pandemic. Many roles had at least some flexibility of schedule and the option to work remotely part of the time. So, some remote working ability for most employees is not a new phenomenon.

The top reasons expressed for wanting time in an office were to learn and grow professionally, collaborate with colleagues, solve work-related issues and problems, and to socialize. JLL Research's March 2021 *Workforce Barometer* reported that a large majority of workers, 73 percent, want to work in places that offer a destination for human connection, including a safe and healthy lifestyle. Anthropologically speaking, humans have an innate need to socialize, to gather, to collaborate, and to build communities. We've been doing that for hundreds of thousands of years, since the earliest days of our species. It's our hallmark.

Aristotle declared that man is a social animal, a claim that has been upheld by a number of social scientists. Maslow's hierarchy of needs puts "social belonging" just above safety and security, and positive psychology founder Chris Peterson declared that "Other people matter."[iii] In a workplace context, the number-one indicator of an engaged employee is relationships with their coworkers.[iv] Strong relationships have incredible benefits, from increased ancillary knowledge to better brain health. A Gallup study[v] found that organizations with higher levels of employee engagement are correlated with lower business costs, improved performance outcomes, lower staff turnover and absenteeism, and fewer safety incidents.

When you eliminate the social hub of the office, social networks shrink, with fewer distant relationships being activated on an ongoing basis. Microsoft's work trend index found the social separation ultimately made companies more siloed,[vi] with fewer opportunities to engage the broader network.

Only 8 percent of employees want to work from home full time,[vii] in part because of this social loss in addition to the challenges of creating work-life boundaries. People reach a breaking point when too many days at home begins to drive feelings of anxiety and disenfranchisement. Workers don't want to be limited, or mandated to choose between either office or home. What the vast majority of employees want now is some flexibility to shift between home and office workspaces and other locations as needed – a hybrid workplace approach.

At Capital One, the office will continue to be a powerful tool and valuable as part of any company's talent strategy, says Stefanie (Stef) Spurlin, vice president of Workplace Solutions. "Of the many things to consider," Spurlin says, "the primary drivers to bring associates back on-site will be spending in-person time with colleagues and teams, fostering company culture, on-site amenities, and ad-hoc innovation."

While the pandemic has proven that people can be productive working remotely, Spurlin recognizes that perceptions and expectations of remote work are changing. And the experiences of the pandemic have led to other significant learnings. "It has disproved some old soundbites perhaps of the traditional managerial mentality – you have to see people to achieve results or to be productive. What we're learning is that actually productivity can take place in a virtual environment."

## The Rise of the Hybrid Workplace

The flexibility for employees to work in the office, work from home, work from anywhere, or a combination of all three has been labeled a *hybrid* approach. Hybrid work can be a combination by employee choice or dictated by companies according to team and work priorities. Several key factors beyond the pandemic have contributed to the growth and rising prominence of the hybrid workplace model.

One is the evolutionary increase in the demand for agile and flexible work arrangements over the past 20 years, driven in large part by employees seeking greater work-life flexibility. That demand has been coupled with an increasing focus on global workforce talent and the ways in which companies can attract and retain the best and brightest – including seeking talent far and wide, and providing greater flexibility in working.

Also important, remote communications technology has grown in sophistication, connectivity, and capabilities over the past 10 years. From mobile computing capabilities and faster Wi-Fi to high-quality AV systems, providing a more equitable experience for those on-site and remote has never been more within reach. Leading-edge companies are considering holograms[viii] and augmented reality to bring the experience of the office even closer to remote locations.

New workplace technologies allow employees to not only work from home, but to work from anywhere, with full productivity and high performance. Cloud storage services like Google Drive and Dropbox have made access to files seamless, regardless of where the employee sits. Workplace collaboration technologies, such as Google Meet, Cisco WebEx, Salesforce, Slack, and Microsoft Teams, have made the hybrid workplace, including remote working and distributed work collaboration, entirely possible.

As the pandemic forced the widespread, rapid adoption of remote working, employees struggled with the isolation, but enjoyed the new-found workplace flexibility. Now, workplace models will need to solve many challenges at once. How do you adapt to retain the benefits of flexibility and tap diverse new talent pools, while bringing people together, building trust, and driving to an aligned and inspiring vision?

Cognizant, like most organizations, is adapting to the fast-moving hybridization of the workplace. As one of the world's leading professional services companies, Cognizant helps transform clients' business, operating, and technology models for the digital era. Rajesh Nambiar, chairman of Cognizant India, leads a workforce of over 200,000 people – a talent pool that is steeped in technology in a hypercompetitive landscape in India. Having led global organizations throughout his career and lived in business centers around the world, Nambiar has a unique perspective on the transformation of work and workplaces.

Nambiar finds that "this phenomenon of hybrid workplaces gets really interesting" in the current environment. "Our clients seek more than productivity from us. They want innovation and creativity from us to achieve their strategic ambitions." Creating that culture of creativity, Nambiar says, will require Cognizant to provide "optionality" of places to work from and in. He finds it conceivable that 60 percent of Cognizant's workforce will be in some level of hybrid workplace arrangements, 20 percent will always be in the office, and 20 percent will be completely remote. Particular needs of clients and work would require people to be in the Cognizant offices, but this idea of options and choice is on his mind. In the company's offices, he envisions a transformation to more collaborative spaces that allow for Cognizant associates to co-create and solve client issues effectively.

Having tested work-at-home *en masse*, many employees want to retain this option into the future. At the core of success lies technology – and culture. A successful hybrid workplace will be built on seamless connectivity between the office-based workforce and the remote workforce, along with strong organizational leadership to reinforce the sense of purpose and culture to motivate employees to achieve business outcomes.

Technology has been a critical enabler for an evolving notion of place, as companies reshaped their business and workforce models, and have adapted at scale to remote working. Out of the sudden shift to remote work emerged a new reliance on meeting solution software, enterprise chat platforms, and desktop-as-a-service.[ix] Many digital workplace technologies advanced from nice-to-have to must-have status when employees were prohibited from being in the office but needed to remain connected to colleagues and clients.

Every organization must examine the priority areas of its business and reimagine them in the context of continuous transformation.

C-suite teams that instill agility, responsiveness, and responsibility into their businesses stand to gain significant competitive advantage. Companies that are bold, considered, and timely in reimagining their future will be tomorrow's leaders. Buildings and spaces with robust digital infrastructure, with flexibility and adaptability incorporated into their design, are likely to be magnets for talent and therefore more desirable to tenants and investors.

The concept of the hybrid workplace is not new. However, in the emerging world of work, many organizations are now embarking on developing their hybrid workplace strategies and programs. Undertaking such an endeavor involves determining how to operationalize hybrid work, who should be in the office and when and how that decision impacts office space needs and office design going forward.

Benjamin Bader is the Global Head of Real Estate at Here Technologies, a global leader that boasts the number-one top location platform, and has aspirations of enabling an autonomous world for everyone. Creating and managing workplaces for an employee and customer base that is technologically sophisticated, with a need for high-demand talent, Bader is passionate about tailoring the workplace to enable attraction and retention of talent as the world of work evolves.

"We will certainly be offering more flexibility to our employees moving forward, giving them the choice to work out of the office perhaps as much as two or three days per week," says Bader. "In this war for talent, we recognize that this is needed to attract and retain top talent, so we'll likely end up with a hybrid model when all is said and done."

At the same time, he recognizes the importance of in-person interactions. "One important caveat we'll need to include in the flex-work policy is the ability for the company to require employees – from time to time – to be in the office more than two or three days per week, for important meetings, collaborative projects, and more."

Operating across the globe has its own challenges, and Bader cautions against organizations going too far. "While I am a proponent of global consistency, we may need different solutions for different geographies and perhaps business units. The 'one size fits all' dream is almost certainly impossible to achieve, nor would we necessarily want it."

"Like a lot of organizations, we're coming to realize that the primary purpose of an office is – and should be – to collaborate. Even with a company like ours with a very significant number of software engineers, we've proven over the past year or so that we can effectively get our work done outside of the office. In the new workplace, there are likely to be days where coders will be heads down solving complex problems, and members of support functions on back-to-back-to-back WebEx calls. On those days, those people should, and likely will, work from home and save the 'wear and tear' of the commute that day. However, on other days, we'll want people to come to our offices to get together with their colleagues, to share ideas, build relationships, and thus build culture, which is very challenging to do effectively in a remote setting."

Not every company will find that hybrid is ideal for their needs; others may adopt hybrid with less intensity than first movers. What is critical for every business is to understand that hybrid strategies are not binary, but rather a continuum that maps the future of work, incorporating work, workforce, workplace, and portfolio. Finding your company's spot on that range will help inform how to move into this rapidly accelerating future (see Figure 3.1).

Hybrid working brings multiple implications for employee policies, the employee experience, office design, office occupancy rates, and the impact on present and future corporate real estate (CRE)

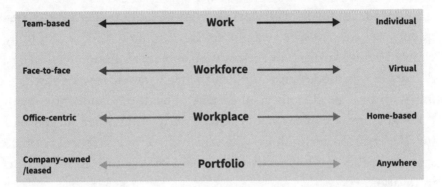

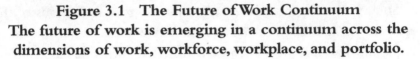

**Figure 3.1 The Future of Work Continuum**
**The future of work is emerging in a continuum across the dimensions of work, workforce, workplace, and portfolio.**

portfolios. No one hybrid workplace model will fit every organization, however. The most effective hybrid workplace strategies and models will take into account the unique needs of the workforce. Organizations need to adopt new "activity-based workplace" design attributes, including free addressing, hot-desking, and hotel reservation desking solutions. While workers have previously resisted the loss of personal space, they now seem more amenable to trading in dedicated desktops for the opportunity to work remotely at least some of the time.

The hybrid workplace model allows time spent in the office to become much more intentional and high-value, with employees heading into the corporate workplace for specific reasons, such as in-person meetings, working brainstorming sessions, and more innovative, high-value work performance. A significant and inspiring physical office will remain a critical component of successful organizations and their talent strategies. The workplace technology that enables distributed teams to collaborate and communicate also enables mixed employee groups of in-person and distributed remote employees to work effectively together.

The successful hybrid workplace model must manage the frequency of how and when employees are coming to the office, ideally enabled by workplace office reservation and collaboration technology. As part of this model, ensuring that the right employees are interacting with one another in planned and unplanned connections with the right amount of frequency and intensity is another success factor. Reservation technology will drive not only efficiency of office space but also the connectivity among workers that is essential to innovation.

Such a model must also ensure equity across all factions of the organization. That is, you need to avoid a two-tiered system whereby people in the office are somehow considered "first citizens" and the people who are working remotely are treated as "less than." Your workplace should provide a sense of equity, equality, and meritocracy across all members of the in-office workforce and the remote workforce to maximize a sense of belonging and engagement and to drive optimal performance from the entire workforce.

Stanford's Nicholas Bloom, a famed workplace expert, previously claimed hybrid work was "a disaster." In his later research, however, Bloom expresses support for a hybrid model of work[x] with one clear caveat: leaders must adopt and communicate clear-cut policies around remote work.

According to Bloom, "Working from home for two days a week and in the office three days a week appears to be the best formula." Using a team-based approach that has all team members working the same schedule, alternating days in and out of the office with other teams, it's possible to build camaraderie and culture even when the whole company isn't on site simultaneously.

Bloom cautions against allowing employees to choose for themselves when to work in the office and when to work from home, because of vast differences in what they decide. Also to be considered are differences in promotion opportunities for workers who are in the office, networking and socializing with colleagues regularly, and those who work from home. They may be important members of the team, but remote workers contributions are often invisible – "face time" matters. As differences in career opportunities and promotions emerge, organizations can open themselves up to lawsuits, with employees claiming discrimination. To avoid the entire situation, Bloom advocates for companies to set hybrid schedules that apply to everyone.

Successful hybrid workplace programs must also continuously respond to how employees are feeling and behaving. It's important to ensure that everyone is treated fairly and able to participate to gain the organizational and culture exposure they deserve, regardless of workplace location.

To achieve such an environment, a strong employee engagement and change management program is essential. A continuous cross-functional partnership among leaders in human resources (HR), corporate real estate (CRE), and information technology (IT) will be essential for determining how the evolution of any workplace program is meeting expectations of the company and its employees at all levels.

Continuous, routine evaluations and assessments can be used to gauge the impact on employees and real estate portfolio optimization. These ongoing assessments should be performed quarterly, to understand where the greatest business, organizational, and real estate footprint optimization opportunities occur.

Successful hybrid workplace programs will take a workplace ecosystem approach to ensure that flexible workplace solutions such as coworking sites are also being considered as part of the overall hybrid solution. Many young employees may not have the resources or space to fully equip home offices, and coworking spaces may provide a very desirable option, especially as they also provide social opportunities. Investment in ergonomic home workplace furnishings and equipment will ensure that employees can work effectively for the long term within the ecosystem of workplace choices. Many companies will consider, and face expectations for, assuming responsibility for setting up all components of a workplace ecosystem for success.

One implication of distributed work and workplace ecosystems is the growth of flexible space operating models. At its simplest, flexible space is space that can be occupied as needed in as-a-service mode, and can be scaled up or down according to demand. This strategic workplace approach was considerably successful before the pandemic, with co-working and flexible space operators seizing the opportunity to provide spaces and experiences to organizations large and small.

For startups and small organizations, flexible sites often became the destinations of choice, freeing small companies and teams from the burden of long-term commitments. In more complex forms, corporate tenants, property owners, and investors are creating their own flexible spaces or partnering with flexible space operators in new, mutually beneficial relationships. These models can serve the need for a more dispersed real estate footprint to meet workforce demands and new working and living patterns. We project that an estimated 30 percent of all office space will be available for flexible consumption by 2030.[xi]

> *"A critical piece of having a winning office building is flexibility,"* says *Michael Dardick, CEO, Granite Properties. "There will be a spectrum of lease offerings within the office market and a building from a traditional lease all the way to coworking. The spectrum will be defined by term, furnishings — how much is included — and services. Now landlords need to really think about what companies value and what they will pay for."*

In a hybrid workplace, managers may need more frequent one-to-one in-person meetings and in-person town hall meetings for those employees who reside within a radius of a given geography. Many organizations include plans for companywide in-person special events, such as two- to three-day meetings in special locations, to ensure that the organizational culture is maintained and fostered.

As author and inspirational speaker Simon Sinek suggests, "Trust isn't formed in meeting rooms or on conference calls; it's built when we're able to connect on a personal level in-between and outside our normal work obligations. That's why it's even harder for remote and virtual teams. It's crucial that we create spaces, virtual or in person, that are dedicated to simply spending time together."

The most successful hybrid workplace programs are built on an investment in the essential resources and an intentional team-building culture to ensure long-term success for both the employees and for the organization. In Bloom's updated pandemic-era research, only 65 percent of Americans said they had the internet speed to support video calls. In many parts of the developing world, the connectivity infrastructure is sparse or nonexistent. Developing digital global hybrid infrastructure will require significant public and private investment.

With the blending of work location comes the expansion of employer and CRE responsibility for work. Employers will need to shift from managing the employee office experience to managing the employee *life* experience, as more people work in a hybrid model. The lines between home and office will blur as employees bring work home and bring elements of home/personal life to work.[xii]

Welcome to the hybrid workplace, where the future of place is more flexible than ever before.

## How Hybrid Working Is Changing the Nature of Work

### Work-Life Balance

Before the pandemic, the option to work remotely – either part of the time or all the time – resulted in lower levels of burnout for "flex" compared with employees who were on-site 100 percent of the time. It continues to be important. Coming out of the pandemic, work-life balance became a top priority for employees in JLL's March 21 *Workforce Barometer* survey. The flexibility, which was already increasing, was a valuable relief from the grind of the commute and the intensity and pressure of the office. This relief and flexibility can translate directly into value for companies as well as employees.

However, working from home full-time has been a very different experience than working remotely before COVID-19. Flexibility and choice have been replaced with isolation and a feeling of being stuck at home. Work-from-home hours tend to be longer because the lack of clear delineation between work and personal time, leading to an "always on" approach that can erode health and productivity.

An analysis of Microsoft Teams data shows that time spent in Microsoft Teams meetings has more than doubled globally and, aside from a holiday dip in December, continues to climb. The average Teams meeting has lengthened by 10 minutes during the pandemic, from 35–45 minutes. The average Teams user was sending 45 percent more chat messages per week by early 2020 than they were prepandemic.

Humans were not meant to spend so much uninterrupted time at home on video calls or on "lockdown" with their families. No wonder Gallup data shows that burnout intensified during the pandemic[xiii] and that those employees working fully remote are experiencing more burnout than those who are on-site 100 percent, and reporting struggles with focus and mental health.

This exhaustion has real, lasting consequences. Employees who experience high levels of burnout are 63 percent more likely to take a sick day, 13 percent less confident in their performance, and 23 percent more likely to visit the emergency room, according to Gallup.

This reversal of the previous trend sounds a note of caution for the future. Work-at-all-times cannot go on indefinitely, nor should companies encourage it to.

## The Corporate Work Week Will Change Dramatically

The 40-hour workweek is also evolving, as employees and employers now recognize the limitations of five 8-hour days. Employees are already beginning to organize their workweek according to their own personal preferences, working the days they prefer, with the approval of their individual managers. According to JLL research, 88 percent of employees are eager to set their own work schedules and 84 percent find the prospect of a four-day workweek appealing. Strict start and stop times may also matter less as the workplace becomes more global, accounting for teams dispersed throughout different time zones to begin and end their workdays as they wish.

That said, work schedules cannot become a free-for-all. Millennials, in particular, report being able to get their work done in fewer than five work days and 40 hours, leaving them more time to get out of work mode. In reality, many workers are falling prey to being "always on."

Failing to set a schedule can help contribute to burnout, with work spreading into all hours of the day and week, leaving employees little time to attend to other responsibilities.[xiv] Combined with the increase in digital communications, employers may find rising burnout if schedules aren't managed and expectations clearly set.

Management plays an important role in communicating these expectations and following through on setting appropriate limits. As long as everyone is evaluated on the basis of work performance outcomes, then the how, where, and when to produce the work will become less relevant.

## Office Locations May Move Yet Again

As discussed in Chapter 1, the value equation drives office location decisions, with organizations weighing the cost of attractive locations against the opportunities that more-expensive locations provide, from a larger workforce to more safety and security.

While most leading companies consistently choose high-quality office buildings or campuses in the best locations, hybrid work may transform this equation. New location priorities may emerge, favoring different environments as new considerations are pulled into the calculation of return on investment (ROI).

Some companies will shift to unassigned seating and attempt to capture savings by driving utilization rates higher. It's important to note, however, that the impact of fewer working days in the office does not directly result in an equivalent reduction of space. Even before the pandemic, many companies were seeing more employees in the office from Tuesday to Thursday, with many working remotely on Friday and Monday.

Also, companies will need buffer space for a surge of staff in the office for training, employee onboarding, in-person collaboration, and serendipitous meetings with colleagues possible only when people are together. Additionally, just as workplace flexibility will be seen as a perk, some organizations may choose to offer dedicated, spacious private workstations as an essential perk to keep high-value employees on board.

As organizations plan their hybrid workplace strategies, some may find advantageous opportunities to optimize their footprints, while others may reconfigure or even need more space. However, the office market will likely rebound in the medium to long term as economic growth accelerates, especially in knowledge and innovation industries. De-densification will continue to be important with health and wellbeing at the forefront of employee concerns—and some employees will recall previous experiences of overcrowded, noisy, and unproductive workplaces. These powerful forces will make it unlikely that many organizations will want to reduce space significantly.

Cultural and real estate realities will influence real estate decisions differently in different regions of the world. More de-densification is likely in extremely dense cities like London and Tokyo, whereas cities like Berlin or Dallas will likely see more relaxed density levels. Across

Asia, remote working is less culturally accepted than in the United States and, in cities like Hong Kong and Seoul, people living in some of the smaller residences of the world will be more inclined to seek the productive environment of the office.

Given the need for modern infrastructure to support digitally enabled workplaces, many companies will seek new buildings in amenities-rich locations. Properties with updated HVAC and digital systems, outdoor space, in-demand floor plates and column spacing, and WELL and LEED certifications will be needed to provide the kinds of workplaces that most appeal to top talent.

In the future, the best offices will be worth more than they ever have been before. Since the onset of the pandemic, companies have been less inclined to remain in Class B properties, where occupancies have decreased 1.5 times faster than in trophy and Class-A office buildings. Offices built or fully renovated since 2010 have accounted for all of the positive net absorption the pandemic and for the entire last economic cycle in the United States – a trend that will likely continue. Any additional declines in space demand will likely affect lower-quality properties in less-desirable locations the most. The pressure is on for buildings to keep up with tenant needs and expectations, or face obsolescence.

"One of the most interesting dynamics will be the divide between the 'haves' and the 'have nots' across the office landscape, where newer and higher-quality assets in the right locations are likely to outperform," says Ben Brown, US head and managing partner, Brookfield Properties. Brookfield is one of the largest real estate investors in the world, and a leader in vibrant placemaking. "The flight to quality that we were seeing already is accelerating now that the office is more important and used for specific high-value purposes. It's going to be a place that people and companies use as a retention and or recruiting tool."

Cities were especially hard-hit during the pandemic, as their previous strengths – high density, public transportation, shared amenities, and entertainment options – became liabilities. Add in higher taxes and overall cost of living, and it's easy to see why some workers have shifted to the suburbs and more affordable growth markets.

However, social creatures that we are, many people are already moving back to urban living in small ways, with suburban residents and employees seeking out urban experiences, like retail and dining destinations within walking distance of the home and office. In the short term, accessible, vibrant suburban locations may see the highest demand, though gateway cities like New York, Chicago, Boston, and Washington, DC, are seeing some robust return to activity. Like New York after 9/11, great cities have proven themselves to be adaptable, resilient, and meccas for talent, business, and culture.

Regardless of how the value equation shifts, the metropolitan area or submarket location that offers the best overall value to the employee and employer will attract the most talent and business – and the largest real estate footprint to support them. The workplace remains an asset to be valued, rather than simply a cost to be managed.

### Remote Work Options Differ by Job, Industry, and Location

Not every job has the same potential for hybrid work. In a McKinsey analysis,[xv] up to 50 percent of the workforce was found to have little or no opportunity to engage in remote work, given the mandates of their job to use specialized machinery, be on location, or be "out and about," such as those making deliveries. The jobs declared essential by the government during the pandemic – construction, food production and service, childcare, retail banking – frequently fit this category.

Regulated, high-risk, or highly technical industries – including government contractors, parts of finance, health care, manufacturing, and life sciences – may also be less likely to explore significant remote work. The equipment and materials necessary for the work to be done aren't readily transferrable to different locations, and oversight and compliance may prohibit remote work all together.

However, the vast majority of office workers will be able to enjoy hybrid work, provided they understand what job functions will be best left to days in the office: those best achieved through face-to-face interaction, or tasks that require physical presence. Heads-down tasks like data processing, coding, calculations, and writing can all be performed remotely without a loss of productivity.

Some industries, including call centers and telesales, may seem to be ripe for a fully remote experiment. Yet, even these businesses benefit from the collaboration, innovation, and negotiation that happens when employees are on site together. Furthermore, employment laws in some regions of the world may mandate on-site working.

The diversity of local laws, customs, and culture are one of the defining features of workplaces in Europe. Just as European cities have had different and unique paths in their urban development, navigating local employment law and regulations are one of the challenges that face companies seeking to institute a homogeneous approach to their global workplaces. In Germany, for example, works councils have far-reaching co-determination rights, which limit the employer's rights to unilaterally execute certain measures, including flexible working. While not necessarily presenting a barrier to workplace innovation and design, these nuances require consideration and management.

The growth of remote work and resultant shifts in workplace design is increasingly being driven by the worker, but it will take place against a backdrop of local laws and ultimately culture. The cost and availability of living space, cultural differences in shared family and living arrangements, differences in connectivity, and many other factors will all impact the adoption and equity of hybrid working arrangements across the globe.

*Nurturing New and Young Talent*

Attracting and retaining new talent with a hybrid work model has not been widely tested to this point. Although it's been proven that keeping set teams productive at home is possible, onboarding new talent is a different story, as is the ability to build new teams, conduct training, and provide virtual mentoring.

The pandemic showed how detrimental this lack of focused professional development could be to younger professionals, who reported struggling with motivation and feelings of connection while forced into full-time remote work. Spending little time in the physical office could hinder their professional development in terms of acquiring new skills, forming values, and building relationships, which could have a decades-long impact on their professional growth and contributions to their organizations. Being mindful of this cohort, and how their achievement gap may grow in comparison to older, more established workers, will be a management challenge in the years ahead.

## SOURCES CITED

i.  Flore Pradère, JLL Research, "Worker Preferences Barometer," JLL, May 2021, https://www.us.jll.com/content/dam/jll-com/documents/pdf/research/global/jll-global-worker-preferences-barometer-may-2021-updated.pdf.

ii.  Ibid.

iii.  Robert M. Rosales, "Energizing Social Interactions at Work: An Exploration of Relationships That Generate Employee and Organizational Thriving," Penn Libraries, University of Pennsylvania, August 2015, https://repository.upenn.edu/cgi/viewcontent.cgi?article=1087&context=mapp_capstone.

iv.  "Employee Job Satisfaction and Engagement: Optimizing Organizational Culture for Success," SHRM, April 28, 2015. https://www.shrm.org/hr-today/trends-and-forecasting/research-and-surveys/Pages/job-satisfaction-and-engagement-report-optimizing-organizational-culture-for-success.aspx.

v. Ben Wigert and Sangeeta Agrawal, "Employee Burnout, Part 1: The 5 Main Causes." Gallup, July 18, 2018, https://www.gallup.com/workplace/237059/employee-burnout-part-main-causes.aspx.

vi. "2021 Work Trend Index: Annual Report," Microsoft, March 22, 2021, https://ms-worklab.azureedge.net/files/reports/hybridWork/pdf/2021_Microsoft_WTI_Report_March.pdf.

vii. Flore Pradère, "Shaping Human Experience," JLL, January 2021, https://www.us.jll.com/en/trends-and-insights/research/global-hybrid-work-models-emerging-worker-profiles.

viii. Jane Margolies, "Here Come Hot Desks and Zoom Rooms. And Holograms?" *The New York Times,* March 30, 2021, https://www.nytimes.com/2021/03/30/business/office-return-space.html.

ix. Meghan Rimol, "6 Trends on the Gartner Hype Cycle for the Digital Workplace," Gartner, 2020, https://blogs.gartner.com/smarterwithgartner/6-trends-on-the-gartner-hype-cycle-for-the-digital-workplace-2020/.

x. "How to Make WFH Work for Anyone," Workflow, February 16, 2021, https://workflow.servicenow.com/employee-engagement/the-future-of-work-is-hybrid-bloom-qa/.

xi. Flore Pradère, "The Impact of COVID-19 on Flexible Space," JLL, July 2020, https://www.us.jll.com/content/dam/jll-com/documents/pdf/articles/covid-19-and-flexible-space-report.pdf.

xii. "9 Trends That Will Shape Work in 2021 and Beyond," *Harvard Business Review,* January 14, 2021, https://hbr.org/2021/01/9-trends-that-will-shape-work-in-2021-and-beyond.

xiii. "Remote Workers Facing High Burnout: How to Turn It Around," Gallup, March 22, 2021, https://www.gallup.com/workplace/323228/remote-workers-facing-high-burnout-turn-around.aspx.

xiv. "Business Needs a Tighter Strategy for Remote Work," PwC, January 12, 2021. https://www.pwc.com/us/en/library/covid-19/us-remote-work-survey.html.

xv. "What's Next for Remote Work: An Analysis of 2,000 Tasks, 800 Jobs, and Nine Countries," McKinsey & Company, March 3, 2021, https://www.mckinsey.com/featured-insights/future-of-work/whats-next-for-remote-work-an-analysis-of-2000-tasks-800-jobs-and-nine-countries.

# II The Responsible Workplace

*"Human-centric workplace design is an ecosystem of optimized experiences and incorporates choice. We need to measure the value of office real estate by its ability to optimize performance. Great workplaces ignite great work. This is how top companies will sustain advantages in innovation, productivity and competitiveness."*

*Diane Hoskins, Co-CEO, Gensler*

A tectonic shift of the purpose of workplaces is underway. The nature of workplaces has already evolved, from all the images of exploitative, unhealthy workplaces of the early Industrial Age that one can conjure, through the other revolutions of mass production and technological acceleration, to the present time, when work and workplace are being revolutionized by the advent of digitization. The work performed today has evolved from functions centered solely on tangible products to knowledge-enhanced deliverables of products and services, with the demands of space changing alongside it.

Demographic shifts had already started to affect workplaces well before 2020, with the idea of a seamless live, work, and play environment starting to take hold in varying measures. Technology companies were praised for creating a completely different kind of workplace, with amenities, sports and fitness spaces, and collaboration spaces to attract and retain up-and-coming talent. Companies in other industries sought to adopt similar concepts, with the expectation that doing so would enable them to be equally talent-centric and driven by creativity.

However, the emergence of this new type of workplace was not without challenges. The novelty of amenities gave way to a realization that installing smoothie bars and collaboration zones was not enough to declare a cultural shift had occurred. Early adopters outside the tech space realized a foosball table without a broader workplace philosophy didn't really amount to much. The culture of organizations and regions, the preferences of individuals in various geographic locations around the country and the world, and the nature of the work itself were all cited as reasons to exchange a one-size-fits-all approach to workspaces, no matter how amenities-heavy – with greater alignment to the ethos and culture of each organization.

And then came the pandemic, which brought upheaval in perceptions and experiences of individuals and organizations. The rapid movement of work from offices to homes proved – at times surprisingly – that there were vast possibilities for productive workers contributing to organizational success from more diverse workplace settings. The possibility of all office work being done remotely has been suggested by some. While the debate rages on about the various dimensions that impact the question of why organizations need an office, the idea that workplaces will disappear entirely has been convincingly dismissed. However, the idea that workplaces will likely need to change and evolve is an agreed–upon truth.

The workplace that is emerging has an entirely new face, an unprecedented new energy, and an extraordinary alignment to organizational and individual values and preferences. It is purposeful, resilient, responsible, healthy, and safe. It also enables a symbiotic achievement of organizational success and individual aspirations (see Figure P2.1).

The genie has been let out of the bottle, and there is no going back. The drivers of change that were quietly causing tectonic shifts advanced during the pandemic, resulting in even more earth-shaking changes. Organizations must continue to embrace them. Despite financial constraints resulting from the pandemic, corporate leaders are now directing capital allocations to this new phase of the workplace like never before. The debate among decision makers has shifted from whether value will be generated from these investments

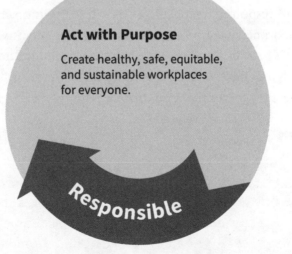

**Act with Purpose**
Create healthy, safe, equitable, and sustainable workplaces for everyone.

Responsible

**Figure P2.1 The Responsible Workplace**
**A responsible workplace conveys a sense of purpose and regard for corporate social responsibility, the environment, health, and wellness, and diversity, equity, and inclusion.**

to whether the investments are sufficient and fully aligned with the needs of the workplace and the worker.

What are those needs? The disruption brought to the forefront the experience of today's office worker. Personal safety, cleanliness, and disinfection catapulted from afterthoughts to a primary obsession. Resiliency was resurrected as a critical consideration, with an expectation that corporations and governments will invest to mitigate the impact of future disasters – and sustainability to reduce the likelihood of those disasters occurring in the first place. The mass exodus of office workers to their homes magnified the disparities between genders, races, ethnicities, and socioeconomic classes. Early visions of a return to the office after a few weeks and months yielded to quality-based criteria; employees voiced their concerns about returning to a workplace unless the company addressed air quality and transmission risk. And the ability for large segments of the population to work from anywhere persuaded companies to demonstrate the alignment of their purpose with the values of their talent.

You don't have to imagine the idea of clean, green, inclusive, healthy, and responsible workplaces as a far-off vision. The colors of this new workplace are no longer muted. They are as vibrant in the eyes of the C-suite – as they drive new opportunities to harness the promise of the next roaring twenties for innovation, growth, and success – as they are in the aspirations of the worker.

# 4 | The Purpose-Driven Workplace

*"The companies that are emerging as leaders in the new economy are truly redesigning every aspect of their business around purpose."*
Aaron Hurst, CEO and Co-founder, Imperative

The term *purpose* has new energy behind it. Purpose of organizations, purpose of work, purpose of workplaces – all are contemporary topics of deliberation in board rooms and conference rooms. All are a way to harmonize around something aspirational, yet achievable; a way to reach beyond the very real but limiting priority to fulfill stakeholder expectations and start the journey of elevating organizational cultures to address the imperatives of today.

The responsible workplace – with its growing emphasis on a company's responsibility for employee health and wellness, environment and sustainability and a diverse, equitable, inclusive workplace – provides the foundation for a purposeful organization. Organizational purpose, with the aspiration to create a proud and differentiated culture, is manifested directly into a workplace that brings to life the higher values of an organization's purpose in all its physical and digital dimensions.

One exemplary portrayal of brand in the workplace is Capital One. Stefanie (Stef) Spurlin, vice president of Workplace Solutions at Capital One, leads a team of professionals that creates and innovates a differentiating experience for associates and visitors. You only have to meet Spurlin once to sense her passion and sense of purpose. The importance of culture, the evolving definition of the workplace beyond the four walls of the office, the role of workplaces on talent, digitization, sustainability, and wellness are topics that effortlessly come across as Spurlin describes how she and Capital One see this evolved world of workplaces.

"Workplace has really become a physical manifestation of our company culture," says Spurlin, vice president of Workplace Solutions at Capital One. "It reflects our culture of being inclusive and innovative and flexible. Culture threads the experience throughout – from the moment that you walk in and experience our workplace. And the experiences we're creating are not just about the built space. Our focus has long been on the holistic human experience, and we are integrating different dimensions of the workplace, collaborative versus heads-down spaces areas that create collision points for people, perhaps on the same team or even different teams coming together."

So why does purpose even matter?

Executive leadership teams today recognize the importance of "purpose" for increasing enterprise performance and enhancing greater workforce and employee engagement.[i] Purpose provides the guiding principles to answer gnarly questions like, "What does the organization really stand for, and why does it prioritize the things it prioritizes?"

The value of purpose moves organizations from business-as-usual to a more trusted, values-led organizational model. A majority of employees, as many as two-thirds, want to work for companies that have a strong sense of purpose.[ii] The emerging workforce, led by socially conscious millennials, has even stronger purpose-led values for employment preferences and "who they want to work for."[iii] Employees today are seeking decisions and behaviors they can be proud to stand behind across the organization, and they will align and engage with leadership who can articulate a strong sense of purpose.

This is not about being egalitarian or charitable. The economic impacts of purpose-driven organizations are just as compelling as the social impacts. Purpose-driven organizations help to create stronger employee commitment, which in turn leads to greater customer engagement, retention, and top-line revenue growth.[iv] Purpose-driven environmental stewardship reduces enterprise operational costs and provides other operational benefits over the long term.

In the shadow of the COVID-19 pandemic, organizations now worry about the potential for the next disruption. Business resiliency is a priority.[v] Purpose creates a preexisting alignment, enabling a much more coordinated, values-driven response to disruption that is authentic and compelling.

The purpose of the workplace is undergoing revolutionary change. The trends have been evident, but the COVID-19 pandemic accelerated the emergence of the workplace as the hub of the work environment and a place to meet, collaborate, manage, and mentor to engender success and growth through individual and organizational innovation and creativity.

The pandemic hastened the natural evolution of the office away from a productivity space to something else – both a learning space and a space to solve complex problems.[vi]

In a world where work will undeniably become more virtual, the portability of talent is a real risk to organizations. Individuals can move between organizations without the sense of loss of relationships otherwise felt in the past. At the heart of cultivating a culture that attracts and retains talent are workplace cohabitation and social interaction. A sense of belonging is essential,[vii] and workplaces have and will continue to be at the center of bringing together the brand experience, organizational values, and culture to enable innovation and creativity, which depends on a free flow of ideas, debates, and bold experimentation. The redesign of workplaces to allow for de-densified spaces that are communal and collaborative will attract organizational focus and investments (see Figure 4.1).

**Figure 4.1   Purpose of the Workplace**
**Ideally, the purpose of the workplace encompasses**
**brand, organizational responsibility, employee experience,**
**culture and belonging, and spaces for human connections.**

The purpose of the emerging workplace has evolved to address five pressing priorities:

1. Organizational responsibility
2. Employee engagement and experience
3. Culture of pride and belonging
4. Providing a place for learning, socializing, and innovation
5. Brand experience

The ties to the purpose of the organization, as stated before, are undeniable. In fact, workplaces are the most visible, actionable, tangible reflection of the beliefs and values of an organization.

Purpose is driving value to organizations in as-yet unmeasured and untapped ways. The domains of human resources (HR) and real estate are closer together today than they ever have been. It is not unusual to see HR leaders in organizations owning the responsibility for workplaces because of the direct connection to employee engagement, productivity, retention, and recruitment. What is more appropriate than for leaders responsible for the attraction, retention, and care of people to also have responsibility for the workplaces that are central to the engagement experiences that employees derive from workplaces?

We are entering into the golden age of the worker.[viii] The decoupling of traditional work and workstyles from the office has accompanied an evolution toward the workplace as a people-centric environment that's all about the human experience. Employers need to build a worker-centric workplace now to better address both the rising expectations of the workforce and the growing importance of human connection, despite the rise of more distributed and digitally connected work. Hybrid work, including an integrated and compelling office, is the new normal and will be part and parcel of the broader way of working.

To thrive in the near future, employers will have to work with their employees to answer the needs imposed by the health crisis and to provide reassurance, but they will also have to address the overriding need for social interactions and a sense of purpose.[ix] With a worker-centric outlook, companies need to rethink how they shape work patterns, while new ways of working will need to be adapted and reinvented to satisfy employee preferences.

The workplace now is anywhere, at any time, with the traditional office acting as the central hive of productivity, social interaction, learning, collaboration, and innovation, as one of many instruments to drive sustained human performance, experiences, and wellbeing. It is the place to learn, socialize, and innovate. If recent experience has proven anything, it is the desire for human beings as social animals to connect.

Clearly, people miss the opportunity to socialize and to run into each other by happenstance. Formal and informal social interactions – from apprenticeship to learning from the successes and failures of co-workers, the opportunity to mentor and be mentored – are elusive at best in a largely virtual world.

However, it is not enough to get people back into the office – in fact, it is anything but. For many companies, workplace transformation is going to be an ongoing process of monitoring employee preferences to avoid unwanted or unneeded workplace investments. Employers will need to decode the new purpose of their workplace by defining how work is being undertaken today and how their workplace can help articulate all new modalities of work. With work now truly boundaryless, people expect a safe, productive, and seamless experience that satisfies their personal and professional needs, wherever work happens.

These rising tides create real complexities and challenges – and not just for organizations, but also for individuals. A high level of elasticity is required in an organization's strategy to adapt to continuous shifts in demand and business conditions manifested in the workplace with just the right mix of owned, leased, assigned, unassigned, communal, flex, and co-working spaces. The emergent portfolio will need to be adaptable to individual preferences.

And finally, brand. The affinity to the organization, its purpose, its culture, and the experiences it provides the workforce culminate in the pride in working for a brand that stands apart. Organizations strive to create a brand that attracts consumers, investors, and employees. The pursuit for brand excellence continues to gain attention to grow customer affinity, loyalty, and longevity. But increasingly, organizations are using their buildings to emphasize brand and its contribution to the values it represents.

Few organizations are as passionate or as successful about creating and growing a brand as Nike. In so many ways, Nike is seen as a north star of innovation and brand leadership, and it has gone to almost unparalleled lengths to align its buildings and its workplaces. Enter Nike's sprawling world headquarters, its 286-acre campus in Portland, Oregon, with more than 75 buildings, and you see how workplaces naturally meld with brand and organizational culture.

In Nike headquarters, visitors and employees experience the brand at every turn. The buildings are named after Nike stars – from Tiger Woods to Serena Williams and Sebastian Coe, to name just a few. The designs of the buildings speak to the personality of the player and the Nike brand. Headquarters serves as a workplace environment where visitors and employees experience the brand at every turn. Banners of Nike sports stars adorn the walkways, and almost 300 bronze statues delight passersby and feature in and around buildings named after and designed with nuances that give a nod to the sports star, creating an unparalleled experience.

You can walk by Tiger Woods's PGA Championship trophy and a treasure trove of Air Jordans. And, of course, the physical fitness and sports facilities for employees set a bar higher than high with championship-level courts, floors, and spaces. And lest the sports displays be confused with mere showcases for Nike's enviable loyalty to and from its athletes, these are true workplaces. Research, innovation, marketing, design, collaboration – it all happens in these buildings.

The offices are bright and open, exuding the openness and the inclusive culture so essential to Nike's brand, along with collaboration spaces and team rooms. The graphics, the materials, and the color schemes all quietly wrap the brand around the individual.

Capital One's workplaces are shifting to be exponentially more hospitality-driven, with amenities continuing to drive community. "I think we are shifting to a community-driven aspect—bring people together to actually create some of the spontaneous innovation that is much more difficult and deliberate in a virtual world right now," says Stefanie (Stef) Spurlin.

Capital One already boasts state-of-the-art fitness centers with personal trainers, providing associates with access to healthier lifestyle choices. The company is also proud of its art program, with art displayed throughout their portfolio highlighting a robustly curated collection of local and well-known artists, with routine changes that focus on important events of the day.

While they may have started as a way to engage workers and visitors on site, these amenities are now finding their way to digital realms. The art program has virtual events that are bridging the physical gap, for instance, continuing the brand and culture affinity for all associates.

## The Purpose of the Office Market Remains

While the pandemic has led to declines in employment and has had some inevitable impact on the office marketplace, in the long term the office will remain a fundamental part of corporate culture as a place for people to collaborate, innovate, socialize, and create fresh impetus for economic growth. That is not to say our offices and working lives will go unchanged. Working from home and other remote locations is now a proven capability, and the benefits for employers and employees are clear.

From the perspective of many of our clients – including some of the most innovative, progressive, and market-leading enterprises in the world – the corporate office not only still plays a pivotal role in the workplace ecosystem, it is more important than ever. The office now has a more defined and value-driven purpose in facilitating essential face-to-face activities that are not easily replicated online.

This worker-centric world requires the workplace to advance organizational culture, and the purpose and the values of the organization. The workplace must create a pride of belonging that all generations in the workforce long for – security, affinity, social connections, learning, and growth.

The imperative is evident, the possibilities defined. It is for organizations to determine how and how much to exercise each lever, each facet, to affect the goals they aspire to achieve. Creating the workplaces we need now will require more than just the actions of individual organizations.

It's not enough for an organization aspiring to build the workplace of the future to load up on amenities and hope they serve as beacons for talent, echoes of culture, and flagbearers of brand. The workplace community needs to come together – municipalities need to facilitate and enable appealing environments, investors in real estate need to share in that vision, and, of course, those who are going to occupy the offices need to want the same things that municipalities and real estate investors do.

## SOURCES CITED

i. EY Americas, "Why Business Must Harness the Power of Purpose," EY, December 15, 2020, https://www.ey.com/en_us/purpose/why-business-must-harness-the-power-of-purpose.

ii. Diana O'Brien, Andy Main, Suzanne Kounkel, and Anthony R. Stephan, "Purpose Is Everything," Deloitte Insights, October 15, 2019, https://www2. deloitte.com/us/en/insights/topics/marketing-and-sales-operations/global-marketing-trends/2020/purpose-driven-companies.html/#endnote-sup-3.

iii. Daniel Goleman, "Millennials: The Purpose Generation," Korn Ferry, July 22, 2019, https://www.kornferry.com/insights/this-week-in-leadership/millennials-purpose-generation.

iv. "The Business Case for Purpose," *Harvard Business Review*, 2015, https://assets.ey.com/content/dam/ey-sites/ey-com/en_gl/topics/digital/ey-the-business-case-for-purpose.pdf.

v. Dipak Sundaram and Heather Barrett, "4 Strategies to Build Business Resilience Before the Next Disruption." Gallup, August 5, 2020, https://www.gallup.com/workplace/316325/strategies-build-business-resilience-next-disruption.aspx.

vi. Scott Berinato, "What Is an Office For?" *Harvard Business Review*, July 15, 2020, https://hbr.org/2020/07/what-is-an-office-for.

vii. "Diversity Isn't Enough: Cultivating a Sense of Belonging at Work." Knowledge@Wharton. Wharton University of Pennsylvania, March 26, 2019, https://knowledge.wharton.upenn.edu/article/belonging-at-work/.

viii. Marie Puyburaud, "Could 'Hybrid Working' Usher in a Golden Age for Workers?" World Economic Forum. Davos Agenda, January 26, 2021, https://www.weforum.org/agenda/2021/01/hybrid-working-golden-age-of-the-worker/.

ix. Flore Pradère, "Reimagining Human Experience." JLL, November 2020, https://www.jll.co.uk/content/dam/jll-com/documents/pdf/research/jll-reimagining-human-experience-11-2020.pdf.

# 5 | The New Corporate Responsibility

*"If our quest for greater profits leaves our world worse off than before, all we will have taught our children is the power of greed."*
*Marc Benioff, CEO, Chairman, and Founder, Salesforce*

With stakeholder capitalism rapidly taking hold, enterprises are focused on multiple dimensions of the corporate responsibility concept. Stakeholder capitalism is rapidly taking hold and enterprises are focused on multiple dimensions as they strive to become more responsible. Over the past several years, environmental sustainability has moved from a peripheral consideration to a mainstream imperative. As more investors apply an ESG (environmental, social, and governance) lens to their strategies,[i] organizational leaders are challenged to move beyond high-level vision to articulate measurable goals and how they will achieve them. While some political leanings in various parts of the world remain tied to divergent perceptions of environmental sustainability, the move toward a green world has very much progressed.

This acceleration of true commitments to and investments in this dimension of responsibility was evident at the last World Economic Forum in Davos in early 2020.[ii] To further the march to a net zero economy, CEOs of companies across the world responded to the call for ambition, action, and alignment with a commitment to disclose and set ambitious targets for their organizations. Various ecosystems of like-minded leaders and organizations were simultaneously emerging with an intent to drive definitive transformation. Bloomberg Green, an initiative company with a focus on the business, science, and technology of climate change, quickly attracted founding partners of the likes of Amazon, Tiffany & Co., and JLL.[iii]

The key difference today is that these commitments are not the philanthropic actions of yesterday but tied directly to the opportunity for "economic growth and prosperity," as Larry Fink, chairman and CEO of Blackrock now famously wrote in his letter to CEOs early in 2020. He "announced a number of initiatives to place sustainability at the center," including "exiting investments that present a high sustainability risk," and saying that this drive toward sustainability will lead to a "fundamental reshaping of finance." Fink also predicted that "sooner than most would anticipate – there will be a significant reallocation of capital."[iv]

Blackstone CEO Stephen Schwarzman has echoed this imperative of sustainability as a driver for true economic results. "Ironically, it ends up being good economics," Schwarzman has said.[v]

As should be evident, these are not philanthropic pursuits. As we discussed in Chapter 4, workplaces are a showcase of organizational culture and priorities, and therefore represent multiple dimensions of responsibility. In this move to the new definition of organizational responsibility, the very purpose of organizations is evolving, and organizations of all sizes are taking measures to be responsible. The priorities and the capacity to invest may vary, but the opportunities to make a marked difference have been broadly embraced.

The imperative to take substantive steps toward being responsible enterprises is reflected in three dimensions of responsibility that are intimately tied to the transformation of the workplace:

- *Environment and sustainability.* While the drive toward sustainability and net zero has been front-and-center for several years, the COVID-19 pandemic put increasing focus on clean air and water in workplaces.
- *Health and wellness.* Capital investments in health will increase, with a focus on the physical and mental wellness of employees.
- *Diversity, equity, and inclusion (DEI).* Companies continue to address issues of inequality, with an enhanced focus on including diverse experiences and perspectives.

## Environment and Sustainability

*In the recent past, the pandemic drove companies away from their day-to-day activities and use of space, providing an opportunity to think more holistically about sustainability and how the workplace can support organizational ESG goals. Sustainability is not a new concept for the workplace, but the intersection of several trends is driving renewed, intense focus in this realm.*

The first trend relates to the nearly universal recognition, years in the making, that climate risk has a monetary impact that must be assessed and mitigated.[vi] Second, with more individuals prioritizing purpose in their decision-making in all aspects of their lives – from jobs to investments to consumer purchases – demonstrating meaningful commitment to ESG principles is influencing profits.[vii] A third key trend involves the escalation of the role of enterprises in health and wellness, which will remain a constant, steady area of focus for organizations in the new paradigm.[viii]

"As the physical workplace is reimagined in response to COVID-19, companies must simultaneously address another global disruptor: the climate crisis," says Brad Smith, president, Microsoft. "From selection of building materials to finding ways to reduce waste and energy consumption, workplace designers today make decisions that directly influence their company's overall carbon footprint. Technology will increasingly play an important role to help measure, model, and manage a connected, sustainable workplace."

Various sources are influencing these macro trends. Within the broader enterprise, leaning into sustainability is a response to investor and consumer pressure in equal measures, as well as a way to address the evolving regulatory landscape. Sustainability is also important to employees – especially the younger generations of workers, who prefer organizations that share their values.

It's no mystery why many enterprise sustainability commitments are realized through real estate. With the built environment contributing to approximately 40 percent of carbon emissions globally,[ix] the path to carbon footprint reduction cuts directly through real estate. Similarly, the workplace plays an important role in health and well-being programs and supporting the social impact ambitions of the organization.

Principal Financial Group, a leader in retirement, insurance, and asset management solutions, is among those reducing its carbon footprint, while also creating healthy workplaces. Under the stewardship of Kevin Farley, vice president of enterprise worksite services, the organization has achieved several accolades, including the coveted Leadership status for environmental stewardship from the Carbon Disclosure Project, which recognizes organizations for implementing best practices in such areas as climate risk management, emissions reductions initiatives and standards, energy efficiency, and environmental governance. These accomplishments reflect Principal's focus on reducing its carbon footprint, using energy and water efficiently, and minimizing waste while encouraging and supporting environmentally responsible behaviors with employees, stakeholders, and suppliers. The company's sustainability accomplishments include reducing greenhouse gas (GHG) emissions by 40 percent over the last 10 years; utilizing LEED and ENERGY STAR® certifications to help ensure efficient and healthy work environments for Principal employees across 85 percent – approximately 2.1 million square feet – of its US-owned office portfolio; and diverting 64 percent of office waste in 2019, which included processing 25 tons of compostable material.

"Our goal is to reduce US scope 1 and 2 market-based carbon emissions by 40 percent by 2035, and we aspire to achieve net-zero carbon emissions by 2050," says Farley.

The rise of the employee voice in setting these ambitions – and holding employers accountable for fulfilling them – reflects a changing situation for real estate and workplace teams. Previously, sustainability initiatives in the workplace were driven by top-down commitments that demonstrated favorable payback periods. Capital-driven decision-making created a defined, often limited set of actions for the facilities team to implement. As purpose-driven approaches to decision-making gain traction, however, a broader range of voices will influence CRE approaches to sustainability.

With greater insights into the monetary and operational impact of climate change, decisions on where to locate offices and drive growth will require more in-depth modeling of risk scenarios. Additionally, the influence of emerging market factors, such as outdoor air quality, availability of wellbeing resources, and emissions factors, along with asset responses, such as a reduced carbon footprint, wellbeing programming, and accessibility of healthy foods, will change site selection paradigms in the coming years.

Finally, regulatory requirements are forcing CRE organizations to become adept at understanding the local landscape and rigor related to the assessing the impact of guidance and regulations on operations in a given market.

Ryan Morris, chairman and CEO, Turntide Technologies, says:

> The workplace of the future has to serve the human beings who work there, and do it sustainably. While we don't know what the next pandemic or other unexpected event will look like, climate change and the global effort to increase sustainability are certainties. Workplaces will thus need to accommodate greater needs – cooling through longer hot seasons, improving ventilation to maintain employee wellness – while also reducing energy consumption. The only way to do this is through greater application of efficiency and intelligence, across buildings and businesses of all sizes.

All of these factors will impact workplace and workplace strategies, from where buildings are located to how they are operated on an ongoing basis. While an increasing number of companies are setting sustainability targets, often with a stated goal of achieving those goals in a relatively short period of time, few have established action plans to drive realization of their efforts. For employees who are eager to work for a company that adopts a strong sustainability agenda, talking about goals won't be enough. Employees need to see ESG strategies in action.[x]

The complexity of this landscape is not yet reflected in how most companies are approaching sustainability. Various assessments of the gap between ambition and action measure the magnitude of this challenge. More dire estimates indicate that fewer than 10 percent of companies have a detailed strategy for achieving their objectives, while more optimistic estimates credit around 25 percent of companies with an action plan. Regardless of whether the low or high end of the range is accurate, the premise remains the same – the bottleneck in delivering measurable sustainability results resides at the conversion of conceptual strategy into implementation planning.

For CRE organizations, this gap can be more acutely experienced. Despite the importance of the workplace and real estate in the fulfillment of many sustainability objectives, CRE leaders are often excluded from the planning process, and fewer are involved in setting strategy. Even more disconcerting, a large share of CRE leaders is unaware of the enterprise approach to sustainability until after targets are announced publicly.

Critical to the success of sustainability initiatives that involve the workplace is the proactive engagement of real estate in setting and pacing sustainability strategy and implementation plans. Where practical, CRE leaders should articulate the value of having a seat at the table in determining the enterprise approach to sustainability and should lead actions that are best achieved through the workplace.

The catch, of course, is that having a seat at the table requires a firm grasp on the role real estate can play in the traditional ESG framework. What began as an investor-centric lens of viewing a company's approach to sustainability can now provide helpful context for real estate organizations to take distinct steps and demonstrate meaningful outcomes.

Of all potential ESG and corporate responsibility efforts, the role of facility management in environmental sustainability is perhaps most clearly defined. Most facility management teams are responsible for direct energy consumption, as well as waste and water management, as part of their real estate remit. Many indirect uses of these resources, such as utility allocations for multitenanted buildings, fall within the purview of real estate as well. Further, environmental quality measures, including indoor air quality, water quality, and safe materials, are driven by decisions within the sphere of typical facility management organizations. These measures begin with attention given to the health and quality of life of people both within and outside of the workplace.[xi]

Through concerted efforts, organizations can reduce energy consumption and greenhouse gas (GhG) emissions with a combination of energy demand reduction activities and greening of the energy supply. Within the workplace, HVAC (heating, ventilation, and air conditioning) and lighting retrofits, building automation, and employee behavior are each important levers to conserve energy, with leading facility management organizations approaching these three elements in a synergistic, integrated manner. While reducing consumption is crucial to achieving meaningful sustainability outcomes, getting to net zero carbon also requires supply solutions such as clean energy sourcing – on-site and off-site, green energy procurement, and carbon offset solutions.

A broader lens on sustainability leads to energy solutions such as monetization of back-up power and peak demand management, as well as on-site battery storage and microgrids. Additionally, real estate organizations should look at rainwater management and water conservation measures, as well as recycling and waste diversion strategies to reduce environmental impact of buildings. The demand for on-site and off-site renewable technologies, including solar and wind power, paired with energy storage, is evident already.

While essential, these efforts are largely invisible to the workforce, until and unless something goes wrong. Progressive facility management teams are using performance anomaly analytics to resolve operating problems, improve comfort, and optimize energy use. Technology can now detect and predict fault through vibration, temperature, humidity, and ultrasonic trends, incorporating augmented reality to train, enable, and assist maintenance technicians on-site with immersive digital collaboration.

New and innovative technologies are enabling smarter ways of managing workplaces in other ways. Mixed mode ventilation and lowering of suspended ceilings are just a few examples of design principles that are defining the new workplace. A post-COVID world also calls for greater flexibility in terms of workplace design and operations. Buildings are in a constant state of flux, with workers coming in and out throughout the day and throughout the week. The flexible nature of working anywhere means building services need to be designed to scale up and down automatically.

Environmental quality solutions drive cognition and productivity of the workforce while limiting unwarranted absenteeism and health risks for employees. Through indoor air improvement measures, water quality monitoring and improvement, and safe material handling, disposal, and procurement, real estate organizations can create workplaces that contribute to the health and wellbeing of employees. Around the world, people spend about 90 percent of their lives indoors, much of that at work.[xii] Improving the indoor environment through ESG efforts might prove to be even more important to workers than merely focusing on the outdoor environment.

Real estate has an obvious, central role in driving meaningful change in the realm of environmental sustainability. Yet, as we consider social and governance elements of the framework, its position becomes less clear. That doesn't mean, however, that CRE leaders don't have a part to play in supporting health and wellness as well as DEI initiatives.

Microsoft, for example, is pursuing numerous sustainability initiatives toward the goal of becoming carbon-negative by 2030. As stated by Michael Ford, corporate vice president, Global Real Estate and Security, Microsoft, "We only have one planet, and we need to be good to it." Toward that end, Microsoft is using its Redmond, Washington, campus as a living innovation lab, testing new approaches to sustainability and workplace productivity, among many other scenarios. By implementing smart building technologies powered by the Internet of Things (IoT), machine learning, analytics, and artificial intelligence, Microsoft has made its buildings more efficient and reduced facility energy consumption by as much as 20%. The company also has moved over 2,000 applications from on-premise data centers to its own Azure Cloud, reducing energy consumption and carbon emissions. Automation, use of IoT devices on campus equipment, green energy sourcing, efficient digital integration with building management systems, and more are all in play as the company advances its sustainability ambitions. And the company is already one of the largest purchasers of renewable energy in the US.

## Health and Wellness

Our physical and social environments have an enormous impact on our health – even more so than our lifestyle choices, access to health care, or even our genetics.[xiii] But with the advent of an airborne illness that upended the world and the way most people went about their day-to-day lives, the focus has shifted beyond holistic wellness to risk mitigation, cleanliness, disinfection, environmental quality, and personal wellbeing, whether you're talking to people in the board room or their living room.

Health and wellness has been a growing workplace focus in recent years and, of course, has become even more important. A healthy workplace is employees' third-highest priority in the workplace, according to JLL's March 2021 *Workforce Barometer* survey. Among workers with children under age 12, nearly half hold their employees responsible for their physical and mental wellbeing, from providing advanced hygiene protocols and flu shots to resources for stress and anxiety – and 44 percent of employees overall share the same expectation.

The workplace and the property or properties it occupies can have a significant impact on health and wellness, and can drive performance. Given that people spend 90 percent of their time indoors, as previously noted, according to studies of people in North America and Europe, indoor spaces are a big driver of health – and human capital in buildings is the biggest driver of business costs, according to Joseph Allen, who directs the Healthy Buildings program at the Harvard T.H. Chan School of Public Health. From that perspective, Allen contends that "the person who manages your building has a bigger impact on your health than your doctor. And this person just may have as big an impact on your bottom line as your CFO."

In *Healthy Buildings, How Indoor Spaces Drive Performance and Productivity*, Allen and co-author John D. Macomber of Harvard Business School detail the nine foundations of a healthy building, encompassing ventilation, air quality, thermal health, water quality, moisture, dust and pests, acoustics and noise, lighting and views, and safety and security. New building and facility management technologies can help companies address each of the nine foundations.

In the authors' view, the pandemic has led to "an unprecedented moment in history – the convergence of health science, building science, and business science is giving us a chance to unlock the potential of our buildings to create economic value and advance health." Many companies are recognizing the value of going beyond smart building systems, touchless technologies, and robust sanitation to prevent disease to more holistic health promotion strategies.[xiv]

Healthy building technologies should be high up on the agenda for organizations, employees, shareholders, and real estate owners, according to Ben Wheeler, who leads design at Infogrid, a smart building platform that combines the world's smartest IoT sensors with powerful AI to automate and optimize facilities and building management.

"Employees are now more acutely aware of things like cleaning, occupancy, and air quality than ever before," says Wheeler, citing the fact that numerous studies show that healthier buildings lead to a healthier and more productive workforce.

"Healthy building measures are also linked to retaining talent," says Wheeler. "In an Infogrid survey, 52 percent of 18- to 34-year-olds said that the healthiness of their workplace impacts their decision to stay with a company."

As Wheeler explains, IoT sensors can be easily deployed across entire real estate portfolios and installed in any building. Coupled with AI, the wealth of data provided by sensors helps organizations better understand how to utilize spaces, know exactly what areas require cleaning, gather occupant satisfaction feedback, optimize air quality, and even automate water safety compliance.

More visible to employees are workplace spaces and amenities for wellbeing. For example, creating space for relaxation and activities such as fitness, yoga, and mindfulness cements the office as a place not only for work but also for enhancing wellbeing. Preventative health care also is another growing area. AXA, for example, has a health program for its global employees that includes annual checkups, fitness advice, and counseling services. BlackLine provides an employee assistance program with financial advice and a telehealth service where employees can access medical care and virtual mental health consultations.

Not all initiatives are complex or expensive to set up. At pharmaceutical tech firm Benevolent AI, remote-working employees are encouraged to take regular walking breaks, while software company Intelliflo started Zoom drop-ins for colleagues to catch up informally.

The comprehensive wellbeing program at Nomura, awarded "Britain's Healthiest Workplace" in 2016/2018, includes an onsite gym and in-house doctor and nurse, a rooftop herb garden, and nutrition classes. At Johnson & Johnson's offices, wellbeing standards set a target proportion of sit/stand desks, exercise, and relaxation spaces, and nutrition guidance in the staff restaurant.

Wellness today has shifted from a focus on physical wellbeing, achieved through exercise and nutrition, to something broader and more inclusive of how people think and feel. Wellbeing is dynamic, and the needs of employees are constantly fluctuating due to life's experiences, which is why delivering a program that covers mental, physical, and social wellbeing is crucial for successful outcomes.

The pandemic further unearthed the importance of mental health, as many individuals struggled with the challenges of the shifting sands of work and life. For 46 percent of employees, mental wellbeing worsened during the pandemic, reaching an all-time low, according to Gallup.[xv] The wellness industry is responding with a $121 billion market of products and services.[xvi]

The Global Wellness Institute distinguishes between mental health and mental wellbeing.[xvii] Mental health is often considered in terms of mental illness, whereas mental wellbeing is "an internal resource that helps us think, feel, connect, and function. It is an active process that helps us to build resilience, grow, and flourish."

Many organizations offer mental health services through their insurance and HR programs, but few focus on mental wellbeing as an additional solution for assisting employees with mental health concerns. Those that provide mental wellness provisions for meditation, restorative care, visualization, and sleep solutions have been few and far between.

Including holistic mental wellbeing as part of an HR and workplace strategy can create clear and positive outcomes for employees. Every $1 spent on treatment for common mental disorders (stress, anxiety, burnout) returns $4 in improved health and productivity, according to the World Health Organization.[xviii]

Although the positive impact of mental wellbeing on employee engagement has been long established, it took the pandemic to elevate mental wellbeing to an imperative. Remote working has often created a "work marathon" culture and employees need more helpful tools, practices, and policies to maintain good work-life balance and avoid burnout. Organizations need to adapt their business cultures, management styles, and technology investments to meet the mental health and wellbeing needs of employees.

A strong wellbeing strategy yields exceptional returns to an enterprise, including but not limited to talent attraction, retention, performance, creativity, and employee happiness.[xix] The statistics are clear – 94 percent of employees who feel cared for by their organization feel personally engaged in their work. Happy employees have 79 percent lower burnout rates and are 61 percent less likely to leave, and happy people are 31 percent more productive and three times more creative than others.[xx]

Happiness improves business profitability by 147 percent. Our research shows that three out of four employees are expecting their employer to support their health, wellbeing, and nutrition.[xxi] HR leaders across organizations must pay acute attention to the opportunities to harness value from their human capital, which is accessible from this focus on wellbeing.

Workplaces had been making steady and substantive progress toward providing physical health facilities and options for their workforces, which is expected to continue and even accelerate, as employees become ever more health conscious. Now, they need to offer more mental and social health services, too.

The pursuit of holistic wellbeing and enhanced outcomes from effective combinations of work, workplace, and workforce has never been more pronounced. Ideally, companies will recognize the ongoing need to invest in health and wellness across the full spectrum of mental, social, and physical dimensions.

Organizations have renewed opportunity to consider the total health of people and consider how they can positively influence new and emerging workforce and workplace wellbeing. The lines between wellness at work and at home start to blur in this vision of a hybrid workplace, giving organizations a unique opportunity to elevate their purpose and performance from substantive health and wellbeing initiatives.

Among the emerging needs that are sure to become *de rigueur* will be the mandate to ensure and verify employee safety in the workplace. Cleanliness and hygiene are going to be key to employees feeling safe in the built environments where they work, shop, dine, and socialize. An enhanced focus on air quality, health screenings, cleaning protocols, and more are no longer optional.[xxii] Employees need to be assured that their health and wellbeing is being protected and organizations must take appropriate steps to actually protect it.

The confidence employees feel from this enhanced focus can serve to mitigate stress, anxiety, and worry. Conversely, concern about a safe workplace can heighten poor mental wellbeing and impact physical health, contributing to suboptimal performance. Holistic wellbeing – physical, mental, and social – is now recognized as essential and research clearly shows tremendous synergies and co-dependencies across all three dimensions. Understanding this interconnected ecosystem is crucial as neglect of any one area will predictably lead to suffering and decline across all domains and, ultimately, overall wellbeing.

Social wellbeing is the third leg of the proverbial wellness stool that needs actionable organizational strategies and policies addressing work/life balance, connecting to organizational purpose and culture. These efforts are proven to mitigate social isolation and workplace burnout, which are sources of decreased productivity, engagement, and retention. Employers are instituting solutions to connect employees digitally and physically, to allow organizational culture and purpose to thrive. Examples of some of these solutions include concierge services, live streaming fitness classes, as well as workshops and opportunities to connect to community and philanthropic opportunities.

Shared experiences among team members help reduce the impacts of isolation. While the pace of adoption of even more innovative solutions across the globe varies with geographical and historic cultural preferences, many social activities are proving to be catalysts to human performance. Engaging in shared wellness activities (meditation, movement, laughter yoga, nutrition for mental wellness, etc.), nonpolitical social exchange and learning/sharing new mental pathways for positive engagement with life, are all proving to boost human performance.

Organizational health and wellness require a robust strategy and a comprehensive set of initiatives aligned to promoting healthy workplaces. Health and wellness are not episodic and effective programs cannot be reactive or even responsive. Programs should be sensitive to the evolving needs of individuals, as well as strategic and aligned with organizational goals and aspirations. And health and wellness initiatives should be symbiotic with the complimentary relationship of society and community.

## Diversity/Equity/Inclusion (DEI)

Societies across the globe continue to struggle with the remnants of inequality and inequity resulting from historic atrocities and exploitation of segments of their populations. It is manifested in workplaces today as unconscious or conscious bias against race, color, national origin, age, marital status, sex, gender, sexual orientation, disability, religion, height, weight, and myriad other visible and invisible characteristics and traits. While many organizations have made sincere efforts to bring in diversity into the workforce, promoting inclusion and striving for equity over the last decades, the results are sobering at best.

A clear description of what DEI looks like in action comes from Chief Diversity Officer Robert Sellers of the University of Michigan: *Diversity* means that everyone is invited to the party. *Equity* means that everyone gets to contribute to the playlist. *Inclusion* means that everyone has the opportunity to dance.

It may well behoove us to rephrase the continuum as DEI in that aspirational vision of a diverse workplace. Inclusion at all levels, and especially to eliminate the broken rung on the career advancement ladder, is an essential move toward increasing diversity in the workplace. Equity – including, but not limited to, pay equity – should be a natural outcome and yet will require intervention.

How equity shows up in the workplace can take many different forms. Personalized controls of space to accommodate lighting and airflow needs, or quiet spots to avoid sensory overload, are just a few small ways that companies can welcome all to their workplace.

For its future site in Georgia, Microsoft is committed to hiring locally, but it is doing more than just providing jobs – it is committed to invigorating the underrepresented, underprivileged community. At Microsoft's Quarry Yards and Quarry Hills project in Atlanta, the company has acquired 90 acres in one of the area's most disadvantaged neighborhoods with an eye on energizing and activating the community. One quarter of the land will be dedicated to local community services and needs – grocery stores, pharmacies, banks, and a reskilling center to fuel future career opportunities. The development also provides affordable "empowered housing" for the community to give more people access to home ownership.

The company has further committed to meeting diversity goals of 40 percent throughout its suppliers, furthering its commitment to representation.

While not every organization can commit to this kind of community development, any can make strides within the workplace. At Microsoft, diversity, inclusion, and equity goes beyond employees and visitors to emphasize accessibility for all, leapfrogging past local building requirements. Touchless technologies, tactile strips, design elements, and construction are all targeted to make workers of all abilities comfortable and productive in the workplace.

Just as important as what organizations provide in their DEI initiatives is what they leave out, especially policies that can inadvertently privilege one group over another. A McKinsey study of women in the workplace[xxiii] showed some jarring statistics about how women are often excluded in the American workplace, from missing their first promotion opportunity to being all but forced out of the workplace when the pandemic upended their planned childcare. It perhaps does not come as a surprise that women of color are even more affected by these trends than others. What other groups might be excluded from growth opportunities, either because the workplace does not support their needs, or because they were never invited to the party to begin with?

Responsible organizations must pursue DEI with a fervor as yet unseen. The debate over the productivity, innovation, and contribution of a diverse workforce is long over. A multitude of studies and experiences prove that diverse teams and organizations are essential for success. A Boston Consulting Group (BCG) study conducted across 1,700 companies in eight countries revealed "a strong and statistically significant correlation between the diversity of management teams and overall innovation."[xxiv] Innovation revenue at companies with diverse teams was 19 percent higher than those without.

There has never been a better time to move the needle significantly in this pursuit. With the advent of ubiquitous digitization and the evolution of the hybrid workplace, organizations have to build this dimension of responsibility systematically into their workplace strategy. One interesting observation of the BCG study is that investments in digital technologies lead to advantages and advancements in diversity, which is not surprising. The transparency that comes from data and insights derived from digitization can be clarifying and myth-busting. Yet, to experience the full benefits of diversity and inclusion, organizations must prepare to bring these changes into the realm of the physical work environment.

Leading organizations, of course, have gone the extra mile, investing in creating presence and jobs in underprivileged communities. Provisions for training, enablement, and language skills further the cause of inclusion and opportunity. Measurement and reporting to ensure progress are imperatives. Michael Ford, corporate vice president, Global Real Estate and Security, Microsoft, states it emphatically: "For diversity, like everything else, what you measure is what you get." Setting goals for representation in the workforce, as well as in the board room and all rooms in between, are critical – followed by a transparent, accurate representation of progress.

## SOURCES CITED

i. Sara Bernow, Bryce Klempner, and Clarisse Magnin, "From 'Why' to 'Why Not': Sustainable Investing as the New Normal," McKinsey & Company, October 25, 2017, https://www.mckinsey.com/industries/private-equity-and-principal-investors/our-insights/from-why-to-why-not-sustainable-investing-as-the-new-normal.

ii. Mario Greco, "Markets Can Accelerate the Transition to a Low-Carbon Economy," World Economic Forum, January 29, 2020, https://www.weforum.org/agenda/2020/01/markets-accelerate-transition-low-carbon-economy/.

iii. "Bloomberg Media Launches Bloomberg Green, A Global Multiplatform News Brand Focused on Climate Change," PR Newswire, January 21, 2020, Bloomberg. https://www.prnewswire.com/news-releases/bloomberg-media-launches-bloomberg-green-a-global-multiplatform-news-brand-focused-on-climate-change-300990305.html.

iv. "Larry Fink's Letter to CEOs," BlackRock, 2020, https://www.blackrock. com/corporate/investor-relations/2020-larry-fink-ceo-letter.

v. Marie Beaudette, "Blackstone CEO Says Businesses Must Address Climate Change," *The Wall Street Journal*, January 22, 2020, https://www. wsj.com/articles/blackstone-ceo-says-businesses-must-address-climate-change-11579721175.

vi. Pierpaolo Grippa, Jochen Schmittmann, and Felix Suntheim, "Climate Change, Central Banks and Financial Risk," Climate Change, Central Banks and Financial Risk, International Monetary Fund, *Finance & Development* 56 (4) (December 2019), https://www.imf.org/external/pubs/ft/fandd/2019/12/climate-change-central-banks-and-financial-risk-grippa.htm.

vii. Witold Henisz, Tim Koller, and Robin Nuttall, "Five Ways ESG Creates Value," McKinsey, November 2019, https://www.mckinsey.com/~/media/McKinsey/Business%20Functions/Strategy%20and%20Corporate%20Finance/Our%20Insights/Five%20ways%20that%20ESG%20creates%20value/Five-ways-that-ESG-creates-value.ashx.

viii. "The New Ways Companies Are Investing in Employee Wellbeing," JLL, January 14, 2021, https://www.jll.co.uk/en/trends-and-insights/workplace/the-new-ways-companies-are-investing-in-employee-wellbeing.

ix. "Energy Efficiency – Buildings," IEA, December 1, 2020, https://www.iea. org/topics/energyefficiency/buildings/.

x. "How Gen Z and Millennials Are Putting Sustainability on Corporate Agendas," Commercial real estate, March 6, 2020, https://www.us.jll.com/en/trends-and-insights/workplace/how-gen-z-and-millennials-are-putting-sustainability-on-corporate-agendas.

xi. Paul-Emile Boileau, "Sustainability and Prevention in Occupational Health and Safety," *Industrial Health* 54 (4) (July 2016): 293–295, National Institute of Occupational Safety and Health, https://www.ncbi.nlm.nih.gov/pmc/articles/PMC4963541/.

xii. Joseph G. Allen and John D. Macomber, "We Spend 90% of Our Time Inside-Why Don't We Care That Indoor Air Is so Polluted?" *Fast Company*, May 20, 2020, https://www.fastcompany.com/90506856/we-spend-90-of-our-time-inside-why-dont-we-care-that-indoor-air-is-so-polluted.

xiii. "Health Equity?" Centers for Disease Control and Prevention, https://www. cdc.gov/chronicdisease/healthequity/index.htm.

xiv. Joseph G. Allen and John D. Macomber, *Healthy Buildings: How Indoor Spaces Drive Performance and Productivity*, Harvard University Press, 2020.

xv. "Americans' Mental Health Ratings Sink to New Low," Gallup, March 23, 2021, https://news.gallup.com/poll/327311/americans-mental-health-ratings-sink-new-low.aspx.

xvi. "Mental Wellness Now a $121 Billion Market," Welltodo, November 23, 2020, https://www.welltodoglobal.com/mental-wellness-now-a-121-billion-market/.

xvii. "Wellbeing and Mental Wellness," Global Wellness Institute, July 2020, https://globalwellnessinstitute.org/wp-content/uploads/2020/08/Wellbeing-Mental-Wellness-2020-final.pdf.

xviii. "Investing in Treatment for Depression and Anxiety Leads to Fourfold Return," World Health Organization, April 13, 2016, https://www.who.int/news/item/13-04-2016-investing-in-treatment-for-depression-and-anxiety-leads-to-fourfold-return.

xix. Marie Puybaraud, "Workplace: Powered by Human Experience," JLL, 2017, https://www.us.jll.com/content/dam/jll-com/documents/pdf/research/global/JLL-Human-experience-global-report.pdf.

xx. Ibid.

xxi. "Reimagining Human Experience." JLL, November 2020. https://www.jll.co.uk/content/dam/jll-com/documents/pdf/research/jll-reimagining-human-experience-11-2020.pdf.

xxii. "Re-Entry: A Guide for Working in the Next Normal." JLL, April 2020. https://www.us.jll.com/content/dam/jll-com/documents/pdf/other/reentry-guide-for-working-in-the-next-normal-amer.pdf.

xxiii. "Women in the Workplace 2020." McKinsey & Company. McKinsey & Company, February 18, 2021. https://www.mckinsey.com/featured-insights/diversity-and-inclusion/women-in-the-workplace.

xxiv. "How Diverse Leadership Teams Boost Innovation." United States - EN. United States - EN, March 4, 2021. https://www.bcg.com/en-us/publications/2018/how-diverse-leadership-teams-boost-innovation.

# 6 | A Resilient Workforce, Workplace, and Portfolio

*"Resilience is based on compassion for ourselves as well as compassion for others."*

Sharon Salzberg, *Author,* Real Happiness, *Co-founder, Insight Meditation Society and Barre Center for Buddhist Studies*

Accepting that they may never operate again in the way they did before the pandemic, companies have recognized that the ability to continuously adapt to new and changing conditions is essential for success. This need also is not new. In fact, at least three "once in a lifetime" crises occurred just in the last two decades—the 9/11 attacks, the Great Financial Crisis, and the COVID-19 pandemic. Each had different causes, and all forced unique business responses and adaptations, but all were unexpected and had real impacts on work, workers, and the workplace. Among the many lessons learned from these crises, and from the pandemic in particular, is that business resilience means far more than keeping the lights on and the data center functioning.

Instead, it means always-on transformation: a built-in agile operating philosophy encompassing a company's chain of command, digital infrastructure, supply network, and the like, and, most critically, its workplaces and workforce. For C-suite teams, that means examining the priority areas of the business and reimagining them in the context of continuous transformation. C-suite teams who instill agility, responsiveness, corporate responsibility, and resiliency into their work, workforce, and workplaces stand to gain significant competitive advantage.

This new perspective is about designing business processes, systems, and workplaces to respond to constant change in an unpredictable environment. To remain competitive means having a culture of innovation, being agile, and being able to pivot quickly and persevere when the wind suddenly changes direction. Continuous adaptation will be essential for success going forward.

As organizations learned during the pandemic, workforce and workplace are critical elements of resilience. Most organizations shifted quickly to remote work wherever possible – but some were far better equipped for the transition than others. Not every employee was fully equipped to be productive at home, and not every organization was prepared to support their employees while also retaining organizational culture and values in a fully digital environment.

## The Traditional View of Resiliency

Whether applied to individuals, organizations, or workplaces, the traditional C-suite view of resiliency is through the lens of business continuity following a particular event. The focus is primarily on data center redundancies, chains of command, redundant power, and other operational issues—not on workforce and workplace.

Typically, an organization's leadership would debate worst-case scenarios and develop potential responses to crises, along with risk mitigation measures. A business might anticipate, for example, a widespread, extended power outage, the sudden resignation of a key executive, a recall of all of the company's products, or a government coup. Traditionally, business resilience meant coping with a short-term crisis.

Organizations were accustomed to those types of temporary disturbances. The solution was a matter of calling a plumber or retaining an executive recruiter, filing a business interruption insurance claim, or moving operations out of a politically unstable country. Address the issue, and then it's back to business as usual.

In the event of an unanticipated mass disaster, the response and the recovery would take longer. In a complex disaster, recovery time lengthens as conditions unfold and require continuing pivoting and adjustment. For example, most prognosticators were very wrong about how quickly the world would recover from the 2008 global financial crisis. The reality was a longer-than-anticipated road, and only the most resilient survived.

That is not what we are dealing with today.

## The Changing Definition of Resilience

Many enterprises traditionally have not assessed risk through a broader matrix that includes climate change and natural disaster risks, failures of neglected infrastructure, technological change, cybersecurity threats, future pandemics, and other threats of a connected global world.

Few businesses anticipated, for example, that a global pandemic would disrupt supply chains for months or that their offices might be closed for more than a year. Today, "resilience" has acquired a whole new meaning in the context of emerging long-term and potentially recurring threats. A broader interpretation of resilience has begun to come to the forefront.

Beyond natural disasters, automation, artificial intelligence and emerging technologies will impact every aspect of the working world and impact every aspect of our working lives into the future. Accelerating business change and workplace complexity will challenge global organizations to adapt quickly. In the face of major, ongoing change, some organizations are turning to innovative workforce models, including "the liquid workforce" and "the human cloud," which will displace traditional enterprise workforce models. The on-demand labor of the "gig economy" provides workforce flexibility, enabling an organization to access new skillsets and ensure business continuity in the event of new demands.

Some organizations also are taking a new look at climate change risk in particular. One emerging framework is that of the Task Force on Climate-Related Financial Disclosures (TCFD), a subgroup of the Financial Stability Board (FSB), an international body that monitors and makes recommendations about the global financial system.[i] The TCFD framework assesses whether a company is meeting its fiduciary responsibilities with regard to climate risks, or whether new opportunities are emerging from a changing climate.

Building sustainable buildings and workplaces may cost more than building conventional environments, for example, but the investment pays off in terms of reduced operating costs and increased asset values. Those building energy savings can be directed into workplace investments that help guard against talent turnover – a perpetual business risk.

In today's dynamically changing environment, climate change risk is only one of multiple areas of risk. Whether large or small, near-term or ongoing, any threat can have an impact on worker productivity and the long-term health of your organization.

Some organizations are building aspects of resilience into their workplace and real estate strategies, and their ESG frameworks, for example. Every facet of your real estate and workplaces can be reimagined to become more socially responsible in ways that bolster resilience.

What is needed now are altogether different kinds of resilience strategies that increase organizational agility and provide the ability to flex as conditions evolve, because no one knows what next week or next month will bring. Disasters can be slow-moving – consider climate change, for example – but still demand action today.

Resilience naturally encompasses multiple levels of workplace management. In a crisis, your workplace team will be critical to restoring power and safe operations, and provisioning workplaces and the workforce with resources and processes. Beyond the crises of today, your workplace team should be charged with creating agile, resilient workplace strategies to provide competitive advantage in a turbulent world.

Flex space, for example, is playing a growing role in corporate workplaces because it improves resilience.[ii] Comprising space with flexible terms, such as coworking offices or short-term leased office, flex space contributes to business agility because it allows companies to easily shrink or reduce their footprints.

## Hybrid Working Is a Hallmark of Resilience

The hybrid workplace model clearly lends itself to resiliency and has emerged as a solution with built-in resilience. It gives employees and on-demand labor alternatives to the office, enabling work to continue if the physical workplace is not available. It also provides companies access to knowledge-worker talent untethered to geography and local conditions, adding to workforce resiliency. A workforce that can work from anywhere, with access to the right technologies and data, is inherently agile and flexible – and therefore more resilient.

As a result, organizational resilience has come to include enabling the workforce to generate profits from anywhere, beyond the physical environment of the office. The interplay of work, workforce, and workplace has become a fundamental aspect of resilience. In fact, many companies have learned that they no longer need certain disaster recovery sites that were once considered critical components of the resilience plan. Given the migration to cloud service infrastructure and the proven ability to work from anywhere in an emergency, disaster recovery sites may be a thing of the past.

## Resilience Requires Cooperation

The resilient workplace is personal, bringing culture and the sense of community to the workplace. The design of resilient workplaces has health and wellbeing at its heart, and employs ergonomic designs, and collaborative spaces to engender collaboration and innovation within its workforce.

A people-centric workplace delivers workplaces that help employees remain physically and mentally well, committed, and able to perform their jobs in changing circumstances. Today's workers expect safe, secure, healthy, productive, flexible, and reliable buildings that promote a positive experience and collaborative environment. Investments in health and wellness workplace features support those working onsite, keeping them mentally and physically healthy and better able to contribute. Smart building systems that optimize ventilation, for example, can reduce *sick building syndrome* conditions by as much as 30 percent.

The quality of life for today's workforce will depend in part on whether corporate systems and supporting real estate can meet employee expectations. Meeting these challenges requires coordinated workplace, HR, and facilities management within a strategic resilience framework. Without a broad workplace vision or strategy for buildings, assets, technologies, and data security, it's far more difficult to adapt to the rapid pace of business change.

Such a framework starts with a broad, compelling sustainability and resilience vision that addresses the needs of the current and future workforce with all its workplace personas and profiles. Such a vision should consider organizational competitiveness, energy savings, and sustainability initiatives, with a focus on health and wellness programs, worker experience, and quality of life.

Providing for resilient and reliable workplaces requires collaborative approaches. Finding ways to collaborate across organizational teams can help improve reliability and resilience, driving sustainability initiatives and optimizing operations. In addition, it can help to avoid narrowly focused solutions by bringing more information and more stakeholders to the table.

Workplace resiliency extends beyond the physical places in which work is performed. The concept also applies to your talent strategies. In a people-centric workplace, resiliency means helping employees become mentally prepared for agility and flexibility, and providing supports to foster wellbeing, productivity, and creative thinking – especially during periods of prolonged challenges. Hybrid workplace strategies, workplace ecosystems, and flexible, on-demand workplace options also contribute to resiliency, enabling an organization to expand or shrink its workplaces, or provide alternatives for workers, during times of disruption and uncertainty.

Ultimately, the imperative is to be a responsible enterprise, which brings together all three prongs: work, workforce, and workplace. The good news is that individuals are the most resilient, more so than organizations. They recover, they bounce back, they pivot, and they persevere. But they have high expectations for their employers, that they will be responsible enterprises going forward.

Workplace resiliency extends beyond the physical places in which work is performed. The concept also applies to your talent strategies. In a people-centric workplace, resiliency means helping employees become mentally prepared for agility and flexibility, and providing supports to foster wellbeing, productivity, and creative thinking.

## SOURCES CITED

i. "Task Force on Climate-Related Financial Disclosures," Financial Stability Board, June 2017, https://www.fsb-tcfd.org/.

ii. "The Impact of COVID-19 on Flexible Space," JLL, July 2020, https://www.us.jll.com/content/dam/jll-com/documents/pdf/articles/covid-19-and-flexible-space-report.pdf.

# PART III

# The Experiential Workplace

*"I think if the people who work for a business are proud of the business they work for, they'll work that much harder, and therefore, I think turning your business into a real force for good is good business sense as well."*

Richard Branson, Founder, Virgin Group

When many employees can work from anywhere, experiences across the workplace ecosystem – especially in the corporate office – will likely be the most important success factor for the organization and the workforce. Yet, workspace choice and flexibility are only a starting point. Equally important is the quality of the workspace options and the extent to which your workplaces succeed at supporting productivity, engagement, inspiration, and fulfillment.

For example, if an employee's options are limited to a cramped, make-shift home office, a noisy neighborhood coffee shop, or a generic cubicle in a bland corporate office, choice alone is not going to go far. More important is the overall experience of working – of having the power to choose the best environment for working, with the right tools and an inspiring setting, to support the day's endeavors.

Every organization now has an opportunity to transform the workplace from simply a physical space and model of practical effi-ciency to an integrated and compelling experience that employees and customers love. With the workplace experience as a key driver of talent attraction, loyalty, and ultimate performance, now is the time to consider how best to sustain and reinvigorate employee engagement (see Figure P3.1).

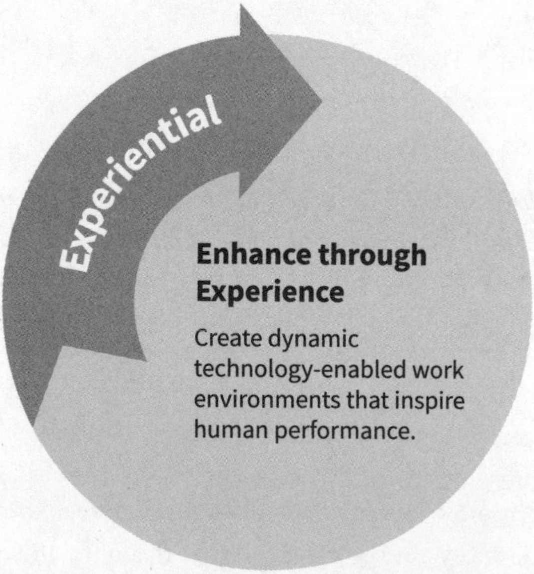

**Figure P3.1   An Experiential Workplace**
**An experiential workplace provides a compelling,**
**dynamic environment with interactive design and**
**workplace technologies.**

One starting point is the remote work experience, which is certain to remain a critical part of your workplace ecosystem in the new world of hybrid working. Our human experience survey[i] revealed that 75 percent of employees were expecting their company to support their home working environment by providing, for example, funding and resources for improving technology and connectivity, in addition to home office furniture.

The workplace experience also involves softer ingredients such as new behaviors, a culture of care and empathy, and leadership capabilities for the virtual realm. Remote working assessments and virtual training for employees and leaders alike should be top priorities.

During the year of "remote everything," companies have focused on compelling, authentic, and accessible human experiences. As parts of the world emerged from lockdowns in 2021, the rush back to shopping, dining out, entertainment, and even travel demonstrated the innate human desire for fulfilling and meaningful experiences outside of the private sphere. In the first quarter 2021, China, for instance, saw a surge in movie ticket sales[ii] and US airline travel returned to prepandemic levels.[iii]

The workplace must offer a compelling value proposition beyond just a place to go to work with a desk and an internet connection. The power of the worker is now more evident, and talent will demand more. In the new era of "work isn't where you go, it's what you do," an employee's quality of work, commitment, fulfillment, and engagement will be powered or undermined by their physical and workplace experiences. Aesthetics, ergonomics, health, and wellbeing matter, and so does having the right technologies to support seamless connections between the physical and digital realms and to streamline the mundane activities that interfere with actually getting work done.

To energize and inspire the workforce, an effective workplace ecosystem puts humans – employees, customers, visitors – at the center of the experience, wherever a person is working. One size isn't going to fit all. Instead, you'll need a deep and iterative understanding of your workplace "consumers," their needs and motivations, and what they expect and need from your workplace "product."

Expectations for a satisfying, productive experience are higher than in the past, requiring more nuanced and thoughtful approaches to the overall workplace experience. Think of it as today's workplace contract: if you provide all the right components of a great workplace experience, you'll be rewarded with employees who are loyal and productive.

Honeywell aspires to create just that great workplace experience as the global innovator moves its headquarters to Charlotte, North Carolina, with a targeted inauguration in third quarter 2021. The new offices, with technology built into the design from inception, is destined to be a showcase for Honeywell's capabilities.

Vimal Kapur, president and CEO of Honeywell Building Technologies, says, "Employee experience is at the heart of the proposition." Honeywell mapped out employee journeys, worker sentiment, and desires across its associates. The various pillars of the worker-centric design bring to light how Honeywell is personalizing space and enhancing experience, while continuing to innovate on sustainable solutions for their customers and themselves.

Kapur describes frictionless access as the first pillar. The employee experience starts with a seamless entry into the office. An integrated, single authentication solution provides access to the parking lot, building, and departments. Multi-modal authentication ensures choice for customers, employees, and visitors coming into the office. They can use face recognition, mobile authentication, and physical badges on touchless entry stations.

A partnership with Signify has brought in digital ceilings with built-in sensors and lighting, allowing for personalized adjustment of lights, temperature, and air quality. "Lighting has been proven to play a major role in productivity," says Kapur. Integration with lighting controls and building management systems enables optimized ambiance and environment based on time of day, occupancy, and other factors.

Mobile apps will allow occupants to interact with the buildings. Access control, space reservation, facility management, building management systems (all accessible through the app) — with additional human experience features like food, transportation solutions, and more — are targeted to create a differentiated experience. The agnostic approach to the design of these solutions addresses the heterogeneous nature of building equipment.

Kapur says that "investment is not the barrier" to creating these experiential spaces. The increased cost is marginal to overall project spend. And "productivity is compounding. You don't need a significant increase in individual productivity for the compounded effect to be impactful."

Not surprisingly, Kapur and his team are exploiting the promise of artificial intelligence and 5G, which Kapur says are emerging capabilities that will be an inflection point in building technologies. 5G, as an example, will lead to an increasingly wireless edge. Nonintrusive maintenance for building management systems, fire alarms, and other systems will be replaced with wireless-enabled capabilities.

## SOURCES CITED

i. Flore Pradère, "Reimagining Human Experience," JLL, November 2020, https://www.jll.co.uk/content/dam/jll-com/documents/pdf/research/jll-reimagining-human-experience-11-2020.pdf.

ii. Andy Wong, "It's a Smash Hit! Chinese Return Big-Time to Movie Theaters." Associated Press, February 26, 2021, https://apnews.com/article/movies-china-coronavirus-pandemic-beijing-e772c8fd5a83a573c7f4749f69d49133.

iii. Joe Walsh, "U.S. Air Travel Surges To Highest Levels in Over a Year," *Forbes*, March 20, 2021, https://www.forbes.com/sites/joewalsh/2021/03/20/us-air-travel-surges-to-highest-levels-in-over-a-year/?sh=106a246060b7.

# 7

# The Human Experience in the Corporate Office

*"Authentic brands don't emerge from marketing cubicles or advertising agencies. They emanate from everything the company does."*
Howard Schultz, Former Chairman and CEO, Starbucks
Coffee Company

Workplace experience and workplace optimization have been playing tug of war for more than 80 years. The goals don't necessarily have to be at odds with each other, but competing demands tend to pull costs, design, and space plans in different directions. The pendulum has swung from efficiency to experience and back again, from the elbow-to-elbow desks of the Frederick Taylor era to the lively innovation spaces of the dot.com boom, from "cube farms" in the 1980s to the coworking bench seating of recent years – some of which would have made Taylor proud.

Throughout that time, many employees spent more of their waking hours at the office than at home, giving rise to terms like *work spouse*. Workplaces often function as second homes, blurring once-hard lines between live, work, and play.

When the pandemic drove employees temporarily to their homes, focus and productivity became easier for some and more difficult for others. The benefits of convenience were often undercut by the distractions of family responsibilities or by the isolation of those living and working alone. Collaboration and team interaction became more difficult. While productivity held by some measures, working at home has led to burnout and cognitive fatigue for those experiencing too much solitude, overwhelmed by household chaos, or drained by anxiety and uncertainty.[i]

While many companies touted the productivity benefits of the new forced model, the reality is that metrics demonstrating employees' ability to still work missed the boat. Rather than tracking tasks completed per hour or per day, what's meaningful at the enterprise level is the value delivered over time. A broader lens reveals the synergy between productivity and experience is revealed. From this value-creation perspective, the most productive enterprises will always prioritize experience with their brand, their talent, and their products – and in their workplaces.

Postpandemic, the perceived role of the workplace has further evolved – and experience is everything. A key attribute of the workplace experience is authenticity: distinct, meaningful experiences, through which people feel a true sense of belonging, connection, and engagement with their company's purpose and brand, no matter where they work.

Offering flexible working does not have to come at the expense of organizational culture and employee engagement. Rather, leading organizations have invested substantial time and energy into creating cultural touchpoints for the remote work environment. Alibaba, the multinational etailer, hosted a remote quilt-making event as a substitute for its annual day-long Aliday company celebration. IBM employees created a "Work from Home Pledge" specifying how employees could support each other in balancing work and life, along with a Slack channel for matching volunteers with employees in need of help.[ii]

In the words of Elizabeth Brink, a principal and global workplace leader at global design and architecture firm Gensler, workplaces should "inspire people and connect them to brand and work product in a meaningful way. Beyond coffee bars and ping-pong tables, workers will be looking for experiences that ignite creativity through outdoor connection, a sense of discovery, authentic and personal brand expression, celebration of shared work product, and connection to shared mission."

When scientific research company Leidos decided to create new headquarters facilities, it envisioned a space that would centralize employees and make its operations more collaborative and efficient in an environment building on its culture and brand.

Even before six-foot social distancing became a familiar concept, Vice President and Head of Real Estate, Facilities, and Workplace Services Robb Scott and his team had decided to buck current trends and create an office with plenty of open spaces. Bright lighting and glass walls convey a culture of transparency and individual accountability in a company whose work is often extremely sensitive – one Leidos team works with US intelligence agencies. In the building lobby hangs a striking kaleidoscope sculpture by Davis McCarty, a visual nod to the Leidos name that is reflected in the irregular symmetrical shapes incorporated into the building design.

"The nature of work and workplaces has changed and we need to create spaces that inspire people to be in these workplaces," says Scott.

Most organizations realize the value and critical importance of bringing employees together to solve challenging problems and build sustainable, competitive, innovative businesses that endure cycles and market shifts. In the hybrid working model, the physical office must draw people in with an environment and an experience that adds real value for their work and can't be easily duplicated elsewhere.

JLL's *Workplace: Powered by Human Experience* study of 7,000 employees around the world[iii] showed that thoughtful workplace design can fuel engagement, empowerment, and fulfillment across the board, leading to higher levels of innovation, and more committed teams. To actively help employees experience that deeper level of satisfaction at work, strive to create spaces that are comfortable, inviting, and most important, empowering. The rewards of your efforts can be profound in terms of true organizational productivity.

## What Is the Human Experience?

In an increasingly discontinuous world of physical and digital spaces, the corporate office will be the beating heart of the workplace experience – the flagship for employees, customers, and partners, a lighthouse that connects and coordinates the fleet and an accelerator to help your organization compete. What works is an experience that is carefully crafted, curated, and continually managed to add value for the employer and employee.

JLL workplace research has identified engagement, fulfillment, and empowerment as the key pillars of the human experience in the workplace.

## Critical Experiential Attributes

Think of your corporate office as a destination – a place people want to come to and where they are treated like members in an exclusive club. In that sense, the workplace can be a special place where employees achieve their ambitions, feel valued and valuable, and build deep, meaningful relationships. Rather than providing an environment of static desks and conference rooms, leading companies are activating their workplaces with dynamic, interactive design, technology, and programming that creates a buzz. Quiet spaces are still needed for that critical heads-down work – but a sense of energy can be engaging.

You could also compare your workplaces to a rich retail environment, with a distinct look and feel, good lighting, and thoughtful space design that enhances the experience and makes it more enjoyable. Or, consider the lobby of your favorite hotel, where every detail of the ambiance and hotel services are thoughtful, intentional, and designed for a specific type of consumer. Similarly, a workplace built around experience will offer aesthetic, physical, and emotional elements tailored to employee preferences (see Figure 7.1).

### First Impressions

As the saying goes, you never get a second chance to make a first impression. Therefore, the first impression of your building or workplace can make or break your success with a potential recruit or a new hire, or even a long-term employee entering the building. Just as a hotel considers every detail of parking, entrances, and exit points, you should consider the journey from home to workspace.

How streamlined is the path from public transit or parking to the building elevators? Are the elevators slow? Is the journey visually

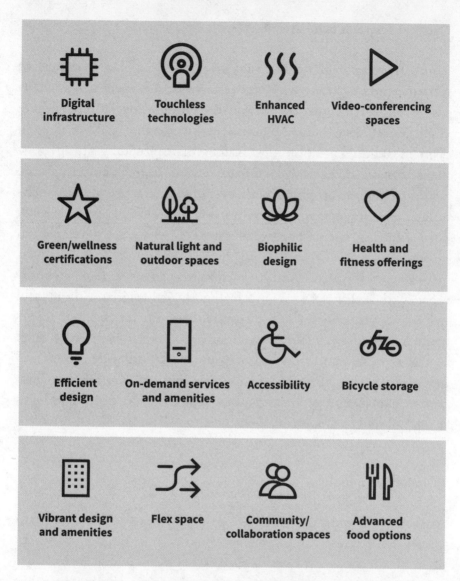

Figure 7.1   Example of Ideal Workplace Attributes
A memorable workplace offers a wide range of
features that support health and wellbeing, productivity,
and employee preferences.

engaging? Is it easy and intuitive for employees or visitors to travel from the building door to your offices? How welcoming is the building entrance and security staff? If your facility is complex, what kind of wayfinding assistance do you provide? How inviting, secure, and comfortable is the space? Are the aesthetics, ergonomics, and acoustics of your workplace conveying a coherent message about your brand?

Taking a page from the hotel playbook, you could consider replacing security guards and receptionists with guest services, concierge services, and experience ambassadors. You'll still have security — but the upfront focus will be on service and hospitality. Front-line facility management employees can be empowered to anticipate needs and make guests, customers, and employees feel welcome, comfortable, and productive — all while connected to the brand, culture, and products of the company. In that way, the workplace experience becomes an extension of the company as it never has before.

At Microsoft's 500-acre headquarters campus in Redmond, Washington, a holistic workplace experience begins when an employee leaves home and continues until they are back at home at the end of the day. For instance, employees who drive can park in a "smart garage" that indicates where vacant spaces are. Those who take public transit can catch a shuttle to their campus building. The campus is both pedestrian- and bicycle-friendly, with retail shops, restaurants, running and walking trails, sports facilities, and open spaces — but no cars.

On campus, employees can use a mobile app to quickly reserve a campus shuttle spot, secure a workspace or conference room, and access food options and other amenities. While digital tools are important, as one would expect of a technology company, digital enablement is only one aspect of the total experience.

The best workplaces engage the senses and emotions with plants, art, or other fun, interesting, whimsical, or unexpected elements – in keeping with your culture – that activate the energy and engagement of all who enter. When employees have a choice of barely coming to the office at all, Gensler predicts heightened expectations for a "wow" moment and a unique connection to the workplace. Increasingly, workplaces will need "magical moments" that leave an initial and lasting impression, like a great product with one stand-out feature that keeps you coming back again and again.

## Workplace "Modes"

Supporting the optimal experience concept, Gensler's Natalie Engels, principal and global leader, Technology Workplace, describes the four distinct work modes of focus, collaboration, learning, and socialization that a workplace should address. Spaces designed for each mode should express your corporate brand and culture and achieve your objectives, whether that means boosting productivity and engagement or providing a more fulfilling experience and giving talent compelling reasons to come to the office.

The workplace must also acknowledge that each of these modes can be both physical and virtual while framing the blurred line between work and life. Employees have always brought their work home and, often, their home to work in terms of attending to occasional personal business during the workday. Now, the lines between life and work have blurred past a point of recognition. Dining, fitness, health and wellness, and entertainment are more intertwined with the workday than ever before and should be incorporated into workplace design and programming, in recognition that work – just like the rest of life – doesn't always occur between certain specified hours.

## Activity-Based Design

In the past, the typical corporate workplace may have had a mix of uses, but not much creativity in providing them. Individual desks and workstations dominated, with 20 to 30 percent of space dedicated to meeting rooms, break rooms, or cafeterias – often on a separate floor. In recent years, those proportions have been rebalanced or even reversed as companies have begun to shift what Gensler calls "me" space in favor of more "we" space.[iv]

Yet, the office still should provide for the needs of individuals. Not every employee has a productive work environment at home and, even if they do, many still want or need to come to the office some of the time. Many companies that abandoned individual desks in lieu of open seating areas in the past decade found employees complaining about noise and interruptions.[v] In short, the office became a lousy place to work.

Even before the pandemic, leading companies were recognizing the perils of extremes, and began incorporating phone booths, libraries, and other quiet workspaces to improve focus and productivity away from the noise and distractions of open seating. JLL's human experience research indicates that the need is not going away. Asked what kinds of space would boost employee experience in the office, space dedicated to focused work was second only to spaces for mental regeneration. That finding suggests that, even with the option of working at home, some employees still need a place to concentrate.

JLL's human experience survey found that employees prefer the corporate office for socializing; managing or being supported by management; learning from peers; solving work issues; learning and growing; and collaboration and meetings. It is also a place to be inspired, and to be creative and innovative. What is needed is balance, providing quiet workspaces for those who need them, along with creative and inspiring spaces for face-to-face collaboration – all enabled by technology. The reality is that most employees don't have full days of individual work and other days of collaborative work. Today's workdays are fluid as employees flow between different work modes, workplace needs, and mindsets.

New types of activity-based spaces for collaboration, recharging, creative work, health and wellbeing, and more can facilitate new ways of working and provide an overall more engaging experience. Packaging physical spaces with a digital platform, and giving employees control over how and where they work, is empowering and a boost to engagement and fulfillment.

### Rethinking Collaboration Space

One big, overarching experiential shift will be the move toward more collaboration space as the most important, or even primary, purpose of the office. Some corporate tenants are looking to the office for "platooning" teams to collaborate on new product development and reinforce company culture, according to Michael Dardick, CEO of Granite Properties, national, privately held commercial real estate investment, development, and management company.

> "This pandemic has forced real estate people to think more like anthropologists," says Dardick. "This is about human beings. People have been sitting around the fire for thousands of years. They are inherently social animals and want to be around one another."

In-person collaboration has clear and proven benefits to invention, relationships, and creativity, and these advantages have been difficult to replicate in an all-virtual world. Collaboration spaces traditionally included closed conference rooms with fixed furniture, lounge spaces, or café.

Gensler's Elizabeth Brink sees the workplace becoming an "active center for creation," where workers access resources, people, and spaces to support collaboration. Employees will come for access to resource libraries, design and data tools, and "maker spaces" for product development. In Brink's view, companies will develop workspaces to "support the creative processes of brainstorming, problem-solving, development, and critique with flexible rooms in which multiple activities can take place over the course of a day."

Toward that end, argues Brink, conference rooms should no longer be designed with fixed tables and display monitor at the end of the room. Instead, collaboration spaces should have digital whiteboards that can be mirrored remotely and furniture that can be arranged for a group brainstorm, breakout groups, or a working lunch.

*"Moving away from many fixed walls, using more movable walls, and more flexible furniture creates huge capital expense savings and fits the flexibility that tenants require to use space in different and new ways over time without huge effort or cost,"* notes Dardick.

## Programming for Learning and Socialization

Knowledge transfer, mentoring, learning, and networking are critical elements of career development and, not coincidentally, organization success. Workplace design can support these essentials, through thoughtful workspace configuration and spacing that allows for serendipitous interactions along with planned engagements. Intentional workplace design brings people with different perspectives and disciplines into informal collisions, and allows for junior associates to informally interact with senior staff. These unplanned moments can lead to opportunities to learn from more seasoned team members, or from peers, about critical company developments or career growth opportunities.

*Designing for Diversity, Equity, and Inclusion (DEI)*

Leaning into employee needs and preferences includes a growing sensitivity to offering workspaces that work for people with particular physical or cognitive needs. Any conversation about the not-one-size-fits-all should include considerations for those with neurological sensitivities, different physical abilities or limitations, or sensory issues that may not even be discernible to coworkers. A wheelchair is highly visible, but sensitivity to noise is not, for example. Something as simple as lighting options can make a difference in workplace satisfaction and productivity for an employee who prefers task lighting or one who needs more overhead light.

Equity of experience across the ecosystem of workplaces also is important. As Gensler's Brink notes, organizations must move forward in a way that always includes people working remotely as equal to those together in a physical space. Meeting technologies and digital resources should be equally available to all workers, wherever they are, along with human resource (HR) policies that don't inadvertently privilege some groups over others.

Microsoft, for example, puts diversity, equity, and inclusion (DEI), at the heart of its corporate mission and builds its workplaces to reflect those values. Touchless technologies, tactile strips, and other accessibility design elements are aimed at making everyone who works on-site feel welcomed.

*The Amenities Arms Race*

In a different era, office amenities meant a coffeemaker and a vending machine, or possibly an in-house café or cafeteria. Silicon Valley innovators changed all that, as fast-growing companies maximized office live-work-play amenities to attract in-demand talent and entice them to work long hours. While more conventional companies weren't necessarily going to offer video game rooms or an on-site sushi chef, the amenities arms race had begun.

Today, amenities in the office or nearby have become an important part of the workplace experience and essential to talent recruitment and retention. One advantage of urban locations, of course, is that options for dining, shopping, fitness, and entertainment are right outside the office door – which is especially appealing to younger workers seeking a live-work-play environment.

Among leased facilities, landlords have become increasingly sophisticated in their understanding of the need for amenities to attract tenants, and savvy tenants are partnering with their landlords in the shared pursuit of a great workplace experience. One institutional commercial real estate investor notes that high-quality buildings in amenities-rich locations will be most appealing to corporate tenants who view the office as a place for talent attraction and retention and other high-value purposes. Access to public transit, smart technologies, and clear environmental sustainability, social responsibility, and good governance practices are today's must-haves.

Amenities factor into the experience and value that employees get from the workplace, and ultimately how much they are drawn to it as a part of the engagement and retention equation in the war for talent and performance. Younger workers, especially under age 35, find these offerings especially appealing, according to our research.

Unique and compelling ground-floor retail, vibrant entrances that emulate hotel lobbies, and other unique and engaging common tenant spaces within a building become real competitive advantages for landlords and employers. Modern fitness centers, community spaces, flex space for overflow workspace, and dedicated conferencing and meeting facilities are all part of a compelling building and workplace experience today.

"There is more pressure now on companies and landlords to deliver the right ingredients for a new office so the right tenants-employees achieve the right outcomes," observes Brookfield's Ben Brown. "The combination of ingredients should improve productivity and output, and you need the right balance of collaboration space with focus space."

Stef Spurling of Capital One says, "The experiences are amenities that we're creating within the workplace and digital tools are enablers for that navigation throughout the day, and throughout the workplace that can be flexible between the office and home. And that is ultimately creating flexibility and choice for the associates and contractors that are in our workplace. It also addresses the dynamic and adaptable nature of work."

The evolution of amenities has to extend to the home, says Spurlin. Capital One is now providing some very innovative solutions that bridge the work@home and the work@work environments. The cafeterias in some of Capital One's People Centers – long an employee favorite – have now been extended to the home. Menus and recipes are curated by the chefs along with instructional videos that people can enjoy cooking at home. The hospitality teams, along with the chefs, are creating fun offerings to include people working from home." They put together date night specials and themed boxes for occasions like Valentine's Day, the Super Bowl, and New Year's Eve so that people can continue to bring their experiences from Capital One into their homes."

### *Health and Wellbeing Amenities*

Following the pandemic, health and wellbeing services and advanced food services became employees' most sought-after amenities, according to JLL's human experience report. Many aspects of your workplace could be designed around health and wellbeing, and not all require major investments.

Employees who experience holistic wellbeing through their employer's efforts report being 29 percent more productive, 32 percent more engaged, and 22 percent less stressed than those whose workplaces don't support wellbeing, according to MetLife's survey of US employee benefit trends.[vi] To be meaningful, wellbeing initiatives must be regularly communicated, simple for employees to access, and relevant to employees' own wellbeing goals.

Also critical, wellbeing initiatives should cover remote work. For instance, managers and HR could help employees create boundaries between work and life, even when work is happening in an employees' home office.

Even simple measures can make a difference. For example, people have a natural affinity – *biophilia* – for plants and nature. Inside the office, simply adding plentiful indoor plants, indoor or outdoor gardens, or a green wall can reduce stress and improve wellbeing, as can choosing office space that offers plentiful natural light and outdoor views.

Some companies go far beyond the basics, incorporating meditation rooms; on-site fitness centers and classes, bicycle storage and showers; or spaces for mental refreshment and renewal. Some have even added health clinics or nutrition consulting. According to Gensler's Janet Pogue McLaurin, principal, Global Workplace Research, "Providing physical workspaces that nudge healthy behaviors – such as internal stairs for movement, natural light, views, healthy food offerings, and access to outdoor spaces – not only increase workplace effectiveness, but workplace experience as well."

Wellness programming should be based on principles of behavioral economics and micro-habits that provide employees with small "sips" of wellness over the course of the day or week within the workplace experience. For example, making staircases highly visible can provide a distinctive design element while also encouraging employees to take the stairs rather than the elevator. Micro-habits require minimal motivation or effort, yet build momentum to create positive behavioral change.

## *Make Space for Social Butterflies*

Who doesn't love good food? Another important finding from JLL's human experience survey is that employees want restaurant-quality food, creative menu choices, a comfortable atmosphere, the right combination of value and variety, and cuisine that supports their health. They also want a space in which to share it with their colleagues. Employees say that socialization space – communal dining spaces, cafes, break rooms, lounges, terraces, roof decks – is the number-one type of space that would boost engagement.

Often a centerpiece of social engagement, good food enhances the overall workplace experience and supports employees in well-being and productivity. According to the Society of Hospitality and Food Service Management, high-quality food service within 5 minutes from the workplace will deliver, on average, 20 minutes per day per employee in productivity improvements.[vii]

Outdoor spaces, in particular, are a popular amenity. Roof decks, terraces, courtyards, parks, and nearby open green space were already high on the priority list for companies before the pandemic. The growing focus on health and wellness has increased the demand for outdoor spaces, operable windows, and modernized HVAC even further, just as consumers in residential buildings, lifestyle retail centers, or hotels prefer facilities with outdoor spaces. The McDonald's downtown Chicago office, for example, has six separate outdoor terraces.

"The McDonald's headquarters in Chicago is just one of many examples of new design trends of physical spaces," notes Sterling Bay's Andy Gloor. "Open staircases, balconies on every level, fresh air, amenities that mirror those in residential buildings" are soon becoming the norm, he says. Touchless technologies, and "private amenities" such as health clubs, will increase according to Gloor, to ensure employees of a safer, healthier option. Gloor feels strongly that these changes in designs will only enrich the urban core locations that will continue to be strong.

## *Customers Like Appealing Workplaces, Too*

The experiential workplace creates an opportunity not only for employees but also for clients, partners, customers, and other visitors to have meaningful experiences in the workplace. While routine business may happen online, an in-person site visit is an opportunity for a "wow" moment and a unique connection when the workplace showcases an organization's mission and identity.

Bringing your workplace vision to life, in whatever shape it assumes, will require the right combination of design and, in leased properties, landlord-tenant collaboration. Designing with flexibility in mind will enable greater responsiveness to employee needs. Office furniture manufacturer Steelcase, for instance, is developing furniture that can be quickly configured for different activities, such as a group brainstorm, workshop, or daily stand-up meeting. Office space configurations could even change with the seasons, allowing for lower workplace density during winter flu season, for example. During the warmer months of the pandemic, Louisville, Kentucky-based Humana created socially distanced outdoor tent offices complete with Wi-Fi, restrooms, and food trucks to enable small groups of employees to work together more safely.[viii]

With less need to work at the corporate office, the workplace must provide a high-value experience to justify the investment in space. The focus on experience starts with understanding your employees, company culture and brand, and the possibilities for creating real competitive advantage by inspiring your talent.

## SOURCES CITED

i.   Jamie Harris, "Reaching the Limit," *Leesman Insights*, April 2021, https://www. leesmanindex.com/reaching-the-limit/.

ii.  Pamela Hinds and Brian Elliott, "WFH Doesn't Have to Dilute Your Corporate Culture," *Harvard Business Review*, February 01, 2021, https://hbr. org/2021/02/wfh-doesnt-have-to-dilute-your-corporate-culture.

iii. Marie Puybaraud, "Workplace: Powered by Human Experience," JLL, 2017, https://www.us.jll.com/content/dam/jll-com/documents/pdf/research/global/JLL-Human-experience-global-report.pdf.

iv. "'Me' Space Versus 'We' Space – Workplace Strategy and Design," GenslerOn, 2011, http://www.gensleron.com/work/2011/2/17/me-space-versus-we-space.html.

v. "Why Office Workers Are Hiding out in Meeting Rooms," JLL Trends and Insights, JLL, February 17, 2020, https://www.us.jll.com/en/trends-and-insights/workplace/why-office-workers-are-hiding-out-in-meeting-rooms.

vi. "Employee Benefit Trends Study 2020," MetLife, 2020, https://www.metlife.com/employee-benefit-trends/ebts2020-holistic-well-being-drives-workforce-success/.

vii. Jeremy Myerson, Jill Marchick, and Simon Elliot, "Attracting and Retaining the Best and Brightest Talent – an Important Strategic Imperative of Today," Aramark, WorkTech Academy, 2019, https://cdn.worktechacademy.com/uploads/2019/10/Industry_Insights_Work_XP-1.pdf.

viii. Gerald C. Kane, Rich Nanda, Anh Phillips, and Jonathan Copulsky, "Redesigning the Post-Pandemic Workplace," *MIT Sloan Management Review*, Spring 2021, https://sloanreview.mit.edu/article/redesigning-the-post-pandemic-workplace/.

# 8 | Experience in the Intelligent Digital + Physical Space

*"Any sufficiently advanced technology is indistinguishable from magic."*
Arthur C. Clarke, *Author,* 2001: A Space Odyssey

The personalized, responsible, and experiential workplace is here, with a promise to power performance, attract and retain talent, and create "win-win-win" outcomes for employees, employers, and communities. Delivering on the potential of the workplace now depends on adopting cutting-edge technologies to create the "intelligent" workplace, one that is streamlined, automated, connected, and efficient.

Much as phones have become computers in our hands, and cars are becoming computers on wheels, buildings and workplaces are becoming computers outfitted with walls and furniture. Work today is digitized, and the workplace cannot be the exception.

Next-generation intelligent technologies will connect the physical and digital workplace channels into one compelling hybrid experience, meaning the workplace must bring together hardware, software, sensors, computing power, and streams of data and information to unleash brand new capabilities.

Before we look at the technological components of the intelligent office, it's important to understand the benefit, starting before the workplace is even built. New design and construction innovations like advanced building-information modeling bring real estate into the virtual world. Digital twins, the digital counterpart to real-world buildings and offices, make optimizing physical space easier and faster than ever, simulating thousands of scenarios to make more informed decisions at every stage of design, construction, and operations.

In this environment, thought experiments are played out in an instant, delivering greater building efficiency and centralizing human preference in the built environment. Companies like OpenSpace are improving the entire construction process through greater transparency, combining 360-degree cameras with computer vision and artificial intelligence (AI), delivering an objective record of progress that can be mapped to floor plans and displayed against dashboards to show real-time progress across time, space, and trades.[i]

Once the building is up and running, a range of technologies will create a single, seamless experience for employees, allowing them to move among numerous work stations, personalize every space, work from a remote location, and continue to manage their health and wellbeing.

"The connected workplace experience will include the entire employee journey from email and messaging to health checks, seat reservation, meeting set up, wayfinding and team connectivity, in addition to wellness, fitness, meal ordering, and other services offered to workers," said Elizabeth Brink, principal, global workplace leader at Gensler.

In short, the workplace will transition from a utility to a personalized product, necessitating an intuitive, digitally enabled user experience (UX) that engages and delights. In the same way that companies are improving customer service and experience with technology, leading employers are leveraging technologies and connected strategies to unlock the full potential of their workforce – wherever employees sit in the workplace ecosystem.

At Capital One, digitization is already pervasive to provide an integrated, seamless human experience to all associates. Its workplaces offer wayfinders, building management systems, data-driven dashboards and tools, and state-of-the-art conference room AV solutions. With Capital One's in-house-built @Work app, associates can review cafeteria menus, find shuttle schedules and track shuttle progress, look up associate data, and enter service tickets. In addition, new technologies will pave the way for increased associate choice and flexibility. Digital desk reservation technologies will change how associates experience the office. The @Work app will continue to add personalized user functionality, creating a better associate experience by providing an integrated tool that supports the various offerings and services that associates use most often. Future enhancements could include enhanced desk and space reservation systems.

## Defining the Intelligent Workplace

There is no shortage of emerging technology solutions to create "smarter" buildings. Yet understanding the entire ecosystem, from building efficiency to employee engagement, requires connecting these systems and many more, getting them to "talk" to one another and "learn" from shared data. To create the intelligent workplace, it is essential to understand the technological advances that are available, as well as how they might work together to power a new vision of work.

Here are a few digital capabilities enabling and enhancing the performance of the "smart" intelligent workplace from a building perspective.

## *Wired*

Fiber and network hardware, access points for Wi-Fi connectivity and the coming wave of 5G all form the backbone of the intelligent office. Without an internet-enabled network, there is no data collection, sharing, or analysis to fuel machine learning and generate alternate outcomes. Like roadways power the movement of people, networks power the sharing of information at the most basic level throughout the workplace.

## *Made of Smart Materials*

Newly engineered construction and building materials can change their properties through external stimuli or take cues from human and computer control to adapt to changing conditions. The result is improved efficiency, sustainability, and experience benefits. For example, smart glass can turn from transparent to opaque with electric, heat, or light stimuli. It can tint by human control or automatically to block glare and conserve energy. And it can adjust to human preferences, enhancing greater comfort and productivity in the workplace.

## *Connected*

Connected to the internet and to one another, the intelligent workplace runs on Internet of Things (IoT) sensors embedded throughout the physical workplace, from mechanical equipment and furniture to employee wearables. This ecosystem of data collection fuels the technology that scans the workplace for information on utilization and occupancy, as well as monitoring for changes in air, humidity, lighting, and noise at any workstation, at any time.

### Data-Driven

Comprehensive and integrated data assets from the aforementioned sensors, as well as workplace and building management systems, provide real-time transparency into how the workplace is functioning and being used by employees. Combined with the artificial intelligence, this data can fuel predictive insights to drive workplace and portfolio decision-making.

### Powered by Artificial Intelligence

With so much data being constantly collected, AI and machine learning capabilities are essential to make sense of the information at your fingertips. AI and machine learning will drive intelligent automation and create the data-driven predictions to both optimize and personalize the workplace.

### Augmented and Virtual Reality

A host of extended, augmented, and virtual-reality solutions will change the approach to space management and maintenance in the workplace, as well as the way employees collaborate with one another to get work done. These technologies change the very nature of work, providing a means to visualize, optimize, and create new experiences across locations. Whether connecting colleagues across geographies or capturing everyday tasks for future virtual training, these technologies have the potential to extend the physical workplace into the digital realm and back again.

### *Managed with Digital Twins*

For facility managers, digital twins – virtual representations of physical objects – are increasingly being used in conjunction with smart building systems to remotely monitor and track performance across building operations, identifying and remedying risks and inefficiencies. Digital twins work with artificial intelligence and machine learning to predict and respond to building signals at every level, from proactively managing systems maintenance to predicting when system failures are likely to occur and taking steps to reduce downtime.

Using digital twin modeling, a workplace team can optimize floor layouts to reduce the numbers of people working in the space and monitor spaces to maintain safe occupancy. Digital twins also can be used to model what-if scenarios, providing flexibility to experiment quickly when rapid adaptation is essential.

### *In the Cloud*

On-demand, high-speed network access and connectivity by third-party providers will reduce dependence on onsite systems. By moving to cloud storage, the intelligent workplace resets expectations for end-user mobility, allowing employees to work from anywhere. Cloud technology will accelerate the reach of advanced technologies like augmented reality and AI, bringing the workplace experience to wherever employees happen to be.

### *Secure*

As connectivity increases exponentially, security becomes more essential. Access to real-time building, workplace, and personal data necessitates a serious approach to cyber security, especially when this information flow is paired with remote work and off-site networks.

Balancing the need for security with access will be an ongoing concern in the intelligent workplace.

## The Intelligent Workplace Experience

These characteristics mostly describe the physical environment of the workplace. Equally as important will be the experience the intelligent workplace delivers for employees, as follows.

### Accessible

Frictionless and smart mobility, access, and navigation throughout the workplace and the digital environment will be the gold standard for workplace environments. Advanced and intelligent capabilities to monitor and streamline users and visitor movement will ease many aspects of the workday through ongoing recognition and information processing, as well as automated safety and security monitoring to ease employee concerns.

### Touchless

In a post-COVID workplace, hands-free technology will dominate everything from building entry to navigation and systems operation in bathrooms and communal areas. Rather than relying on touch, the workplace will be powered by voice, hand gestures, user behavior, facial recognition, and other physical movement signals.

### App-enabled

Employees will get the best of their workplace, right on their phone. From navigating workplace environments to connecting with co-workers and the array of amenities and services offered, the workplace app will connect everything that is available to the workforce through-out the digital and physical realm. This one-stop system also provides a single source to gather workplace data and feed building management systems.

### Consumer Workplace Experience

Like logging on to a great retail site, the workplace app will help workers navigate to the vendors, amenities, tools, and products they need and desire, whether that's to fuel their work or to help them take a well-deserved break.

### Digitally Reserved

Never spend time circling the parking lot again. Smart booking systems give employees the opportunity to reserve a parking spot, a desk, a room, and much more. Synched to an occupancy management system to constantly optimize the workplace, digital reservations ensure every employee has the right space near the right people to fuel their workday.

### Collaborative

Whether on site or remote, employees can connect seamlessly with their teams across workplace channels, including digitally facilitating planned and spontaneous interactions.

Virtual and in-person meeting technology will make teams more connected than ever. Beyond video cameras and top-notch sound systems, the next generation of virtual meetings will combine video-conference screens and software, digital walls, holograms, projections, and other immersive meeting technology.

Of course, the real magic of the hybrid workplace and the technology that powers it is the way building systems and human experience connect with and engage one another. Rather than a static list of new technology, the intelligent workplace will constantly compound, leveraging new technology developments and creating a workplace that is more than a location, but rather an ecosystem of amenities and experiences that cross the physical and digital divide.

Picture the last time you went into an Apple retail store. You didn't go stalking aisles looking for the particular product. You likely noticed the experiential components: short classes and training taking place in open forums; demonstrations and conversations happening in small groups over low, glass cases; new products to toy with and feel for yourself. Products aren't segmented by what they are – computers, accessories, and power sources – but by their purpose of bringing music, fitness, and connection into every realm of life.

You don't pluck an Apple product off the shelf, but rather, visit the store to hold it in your hand and purchase your product from an associate or online. You can order from home and pick it up curbside. There are no lines or harried store employees. Customer service and customer experience are at the center of the Apple retail experience.

This omnichannel approach is coming for the workplace, providing multiple channels to drive productivity and enhance experience, with convergent technologies powering connection throughout the business world. Workplace consumer needs will no longer be solved through a series of interdepartmental steps, but rather, through the tap of an app on a smartphone.

## The New Hybrid, Intelligent, and Digitized Workplace Is Here

These capabilities are not a futuristic or forecasted workplace technology – they are already here, just not yet evenly distributed. Digital capabilities are accelerating and quickly shifting from "nice-to-have" to "must-have" for building owners and corporate real estate occupiers. Ninety-eight percent of office workers say they would not be able to do their job with the same level of ease without technology, according to a 2021 global survey conducted by WiredScore and Opinium Research.[ii]

Leading organizations such as Accenture, Apple, Facebook, Google, Honeywell, JLL, Microsoft, and PwC have already blurred the digital intelligence of emerging technologies with the physical workplace experience, creating a new "phygital" approach to work.

> In the heart of London, management consultancy and research firm UnWork is advising the developer of 22 Bishopsgate, which will be London's smartest building once complete. The building is equipped with biometric identification systems that power touchless entry and elevator calls. An app from Smart Spaces will guide employees to their suite and enable a frictionless visitor experience with the app telling them exactly where to go. Cell phones unlock the workplace experience, acting as a universal remote to contact building systems, responding to individual needs in shaping a unique workplace journey.
>
> "The key prediction is that space will have the intelligence to know who is there, what they want to do, and how best to enable an experience. The automation of physical environments will have profound impacts for building owners and exciting opportunities for new developments," says Phillip Ross, CEO of UnWork.

The building follows from the pioneering work by The Edge in Amsterdam,[iii] dubbed "the smartest building in the world," creating real estate that knows everything about its inhabitants, from where they like to park to how they take their coffee, and uses that intelligence to power two-way interaction and control the physical spaces that surround them.

Workplace technologies, including smart sensors, are powering these developments that "know" when someone is present in the physical workplace. They make it possible to personalize controls, giving employees the power to shape or "tune" the environment to meet their needs. Personalization includes being able to adjust temperature or change the lighting to improve performance. And the terabytes of data produced from these sensors create new potential for intelligent operation of real estate assets.

Within the building, often unseen, an even greater number of new technologies are emerging, further powering this symbiotic relationship between workplace and workforce.

## Innovative Real Estate Solutions Keep Expanding

Technology for real estate has grown quickly in size and complexity over the past decade, with an estimated 8,000 to 10,000 companies now offering technology-focused solutions across the global built environment, according to our research. This represents a massive increase in an industry that has been traditionally slow to adapt and innovate.

Property technology (proptech) startups can now be found in most countries around the world, and many of the more established technology companies in the sector have global operations and reach. In the US alone, which has the largest and most mature proptech ecosystem, startups focused on real estate raised $16.6 billion of venture capital funding in 2019 and another $10 billion in 2020, despite the pandemic. The expanding ecosystem of real estate technology today encompasses innovative material, hardware, software, and digital connectivity.

Companies like Turntide Technologies are focusing on the most basic building blocks of building technology: in this case, a smarter electric motor. The company has spent more than a decade perfecting a new kind of software-controlled motor that pulses electricity, rather than providing a constant current, to control the speed of operation. The difference between those two methods can reduce energy consumption by 64 percent.[iv] If Turntide's motor replaced all the motors in buildings throughout the US, that would be the equivalent of capturing 300 million tons of atmospheric carbon per year.

Turntide's hardware has garnered well-deserved accolades, but the real secret to its success is the myriad of sensors and software that continuously optimize the engine's output. Connected to the cloud, the motor continuously transmits real-time data for remote monitoring, with faults and signs of degradation detected at the earliest possible moment.[v]

The ongoing monitoring, management, and control of building systems will continue to generate new technology solutions, while startups like HqO, Rise, and Lane are targeting property owners with capabilities that improve access, amenities, communication, and engagement at the property, workplace, and tenant levels.

Smart building systems can enable smart workspaces and further support the employee experience – and also contribute to sustainability goals. Generally speaking, buildings with advanced technology are better suited to support environmental, sustainability, health, and wellness initiatives, and they offer the employees who work in them a better overall experience.

Through automated, ongoing adjustments, smart building systems help maintain indoor air quality and comfortable temperatures, and their smart-workplace efficiency reduces energy waste and extends equipment life. For the people-centric workplace, smart building systems can power personalized workspace controls to put employees in charge of their environments – and reduce the all-too-common complaints about the office being too hot or too cold, too brightly lit or lacking task lighting.

These products are enhancing the digital experience within the workplace, enabling data-driven decision-making. Many corporate real estate (CRE) teams are building or partnering on their own workplace apps as well to bridge the distributed and complex workplace ecosystem.

As we have seen, one evolution of this capability will be the use of voice commands to control the space around us. JLL Jet is an example of an intelligent mobile workplace app that leverages voice-recognition and artificial intelligence (AI) technology for workplace navigation, reservation, and support, bringing the ease and simplicity of Siri or Alexa to the workplace for daily needs, from space reservations to getting answers to frequently asked questions.[vi]

We will begin to see the evolution of intelligent, self-organizing, and automatic CRE portfolio optimization platforms that will further adapt to meet the continuous changing demand cycles of the hybrid workforce, which will bring new patterns and activities that change day by day. Today's workplace utilization data and analytics tools can be used to monitor workplace use to ensure you're providing the right mix of workspaces for current needs and preferences.

For example, organizations can use sensors, Wi-Fi data, security badge swipes, and other sources to gather data about where and when employees are working, and then leverage analytical tools to predict future space needs. Sensor data can be fed to an integrated workplace management system (IWMS) and enterprise systems such as Workday, Oracle, Microsoft, SAP, and others.

These technologies accommodate transformative planning methods like dynamic zones and micro-supply/demand management, brought to life via AI, smart space assignments, and utilization data. Through AI, an automated system can "know" many workers will need what type of space and assign it through software algorithms, accounting for volume, space preferences, and tools required to improve productivity.[vii] All will be provisioned in a seamless and intelligent manner that can be updated on a weekly, daily, and even hourly basis. When seat selection guesswork is removed, employees can more easily collaborate in person.[viii]

The insights derived from building and workplace data can help organizations fine-tune space utilization on an ongoing basis and right-size your real estate footprint. If people are overbooking the conference rooms, for instance, while open spaces are underutilized, it may be wise to repurpose space into additional meeting rooms. By tracking not just meeting room bookings but occupancy throughout the day, you can learn whether every meeting room seat is occupied all day – or whether employees are hiding out in the conference room because few quiet workspace options are available.

Dynamic occupancy planning holds the promise to reduce occupancy costs and improve the employee experience by removing the confusion and guesswork surrounding seat selection. It's a "win–win" scenario that can create on-demand space use and maximize the value of each component of the workplace.

The intelligent workplace is, by definition, enabled by AI, powering the software and systems that help organizations manage their workplace. It is a critical piece of the puzzle that will enable dynamic workplaces, flexible portfolios, and environments that enhance human performance.

Proptech partners such as GoSpace and VergeSense are using AI to provide new capabilities to monitor and map real-time occupancy and utilization. GoSpace balances the supply of workspace with fluctuating demand, to eliminate midweek crowding and reduce real estate costs by helping occupiers understand exactly how much space they need. The VergeSense platform combines best-in-class optical sensors, a scalable analytics tool, and expert guidance to identify curated insights on workplace utilization to fuel workplace management systems, space reservation systems, and other digital workplace tools.

According to Dan Ryan, CEO of VergeSense, "Workplace analytics platforms and sensor technology like VergeSense will be a staple for competitive business, and the outcome will be fast, confident choices in real estate decisions and office layout and design that drive the most productive and effective culture and working environments."

"We should be seeing how our buildings are functioning, how spaces are really used, how our air filtration is working, and how much natural air is circulating," says Natalie Engels, principal and global leader, Technology Workplace at Gensler. "Data plays a large role in design optimization and resilience, building operations, and the human experience in offices."

"Workplace apps for wayfinding, food ordering, building culture and connecting are now the hot item that so many companies are trying to create or leveraging digital experience design teams to create," Engels says. "This allows for a seamlessly integrated employee experience with tailored apps and companywide communication that will suit both individual needs, team dynamics, and how tenants lease space."

Of course, realizing this vision of a seamlessly intertwined and connected hybrid workplace will not happen automatically. Real estate leaders must be aware of the potential pitfalls that will appear as the new intelligent workplace emerges.

## The Challenges of a Hybrid Environment

Workplace technologies will amplify efficient operations and inefficient operations in equal measure. Technology cannot solve for existing systems that don't prioritize human experience and ease of use.

One of the greatest challenges to powering the hybrid workplace is not technology at all, but bringing together the people – building owners, property managers, tenants, CRE leaders, HR, individual employees – to understand needs and limitations. There must be a culture of experimentation that allows all parties to pilot, test, learn, adapt, and integrate new technology solutions. This complex crossover of roles and outlooks is essential for bringing the full force of the hybrid workplace to life. No one party can do it alone.

Only once the people are involved in shaping the workplace experience can the technology come into play. Finding the right technology tools, integrating them, and continuing to provide a seamless and connected experience will be an always-on operation.

Progress will necessitate a combination of in-house technology capabilities and collaboration across the real estate owner and occupier businesses and with proptech companies, many of which are taking a scattered approach to offering new solutions. Some proptech companies have grown exponentially, especially as the need for a more digitally connected workplace emerged throughout the pandemic, but, in many cases, they are still trying to map effectively to customer needs and drive adoption at scale.

The heterogenous nature of the built environment means that it can be difficult to develop and deploy common approaches, industry standards, and applications across geographies and properties. Narrow focus and limited use of emerging proptech can result in a scattershot approach to connectivity, with new solutions emerging and being consolidated at a quickening pace. The proptech industry landscape is highly fragmented, making it difficult for companies to navigate and stay educated on options, find the best solution or provider or vendor for their needs, and then effectively deploy new technologies. The situation can be a significant source of frustration among decision makers and end users alike, resulting in longer decision cycles, slower adoption, and missed opportunities.

The hybrid workplace itself will need time to settle before it can be fully navigated and assessed, though capturing and analyzing more data will help improve workplace decision making. An array of opportunities and pain points will be revealed over time. Many organizations are still undecided about exactly where their workplace policies and programs will land in the coming years, meaning that an agile and continual learning approach will be essential as employees return to the workplace in some capacity. As companies and employees learn more about what works and what does not for their specific situation, technology will arm them with new tools and dashboards to monitor, engage, model, and implement potential adjustments and adaptations to continually improve the experience and efficiency of the workplace.

> "Workspaces will always be different for different organizations. One thing is for certain, that without data and taking the leap of digital transformation, companies will struggle to make the right decisions around the space that is truly responsive to people," says Shagufta Anurag, CEO of Saltmine, a real estate technology startup transforming the workplace design process.

Intelligent capabilities can help overcome challenges in the new work setting. People will expect a range of new and intuitive innovations, including accessing the various work settings, schedules, reservations, and amenities of the workplace ecosystem, all of which are essential to enabling a safe, productive, and healthy workplace experience.

For example, creating equal opportunity and experiences across in-person and remote teams will be critical in the early days of hybrid, as will empowering teams that are at different comfort levels with new technology. Distributed, multigenerational, and more liquid workforces, with a mix of full-time employees and contract or gig workers, are likely to bring this challenge to light. Just as the office is becoming a network of workplace options, the workforce is becoming increasingly flexible. In some organizations, more employees have become contingent, contract labor – sometimes referred to as the "human cloud." How will all of these individual needs be addressed through new technology and workplace policies?

Technology should enable hybrid experiences across the entire workforce ecosystem, but even some of the basic "blended" environments pose risks.

"Blended reality and technology-enabled conference will be essential to furthering collaboration with dispersed teams," says Gensler's Natalie Engels. "We saw before the pandemic that it is always a challenge with teams working globally. It will be even more so now, and not just in the way it used to be."

"The people who are working remotely will all be on equal ground, equal face size, equal voice, and the people within a room will be smaller, talking to one another. As soon as someone in the room is not inclusive, two meetings are then taking place. We must be mindful of behaviors that could be created and work to eliminate them. The technology, the practices put in place, the furniture set up, the ability to mirror whiteboarding will be more important to think through than ever before."

The issue of inclusion is no less important when considering spontaneous interactions among employees and across teams, the kind that often spark ideation and creation. The interactions are critical for building trust, relationships, and culture. Digital capabilities can and must be deployed to create these unexpected collisions and collaborations, even for those who are not often on planned web calls or all-hands meetings.

"The tools exist to have a coffee break in the office with someone in the office café, someone in their kitchen at home, and another person waiting for their flight at an airport," Engels said. "The pandemic has given us the acceptability for that behavior to exist and an acceleration in the seamlessness of the technology. Organizations that invest in these tools and integrate them into the design of the office will have a leading edge."

Clearly, our view is that the benefits of the intelligent workplace outweigh any potential challenges.

"There is an incredible opportunity to fix what wasn't working in the office prepandemic," says Janet Pogue McLaurin, principal, global workplace research leader at Gensler. "In Gensler's 2013 research, we found that employers who provide a spectrum of choices for when and where to work were seen as more innovative and have higher-performing employees. In 2016, we found that innovative companies spend more time collaborating away from their desk and spend only about 3.5 days of their workweek in the office. This shows our research has consistently proven that people who work one or two days away from the office have a better experience, higher workplace satisfaction, and higher job commitment – all indicators of higher employee engagement."

There's never been a more exciting time to shape the workplace environment, but with all these possibilities comes enormous responsibility. A tech-enabled hybrid workplace has the potential to unleash workforce creativity and productivity like never before. It deserves a thoughtful plan, created with trusted and experienced partners, to help set your organization on the path to success.

## SOURCES CITED

i.  Carla Lauter, "OpenSpace Expands AI-Backed Progress Tracking to Coordinate Across Trades," SPAR 3D, April 20, 2021, https://www.spar3d.com/news/aec/openspace-expands-ai-backed-progress-tracking-to-coordinate-projects-across-trades/.

ii.  "Smart Buildings: Our Future Is Smart," SmartScore, April 2021, https://wiredscore.com/wp-content/uploads/2021/04/2021-Smart-Building-Whitepaper.pdf.

iii.  Tom Randall, "The Smartest Building in the World," Bloomberg, September 23, 2015, https://www.bloomberg.com/features/2015-the-edge-the-worlds-greenest-building/.

iv.  Jonathan Shieber, "Firms Backed by Robert Downey Jr. and Bill Gates Have Funded an Electric Motor Company That Slashes Energy Consumption,"

World Economic Forum, March 5, 2021, https://www.weforum.org/agenda/2021/03/firms-backed-by-robert-downey-jr-and-bill-gates-have-funded-an-electric-motor-company-that-slashes-energy-consumption/.

v. "How Smart Electric Motors Could Reduce Carbon Emissions," *Nanalyze,* March 16, 2021, https://www.nanalyze.com/2020/11/smart-electric-motors/.

vi. Martin Giles, "Microsoft's $19.7 Billion Nuance Deal Comes as CIOs Tap Voice AI to Help Customers and Workers," *Forbes,* April 14, 2021, https://www.forbes.com/sites/martingiles/2021/04/12/microsofts-nuance-deal-comes-as-cios-rely-on-voice-ai/?sh=2fbda4c1637e.

vii. Cynthia Kantor, "Artificial Intelligence Is Making the Workplace of Tomorrow More Human than Ever," CoreNet Global's The Pulse, March 16, 2021, https://blog.corenetglobal.org/blog/artificial-intelligence-is-making-the-workplace-of-tomorrow-more-human-than-ever/.

viii. *Dynamic Occupancy Planning,* JLL, 2021, https://www.us.jll.com/en/products/dynamic-op.

# PART IV | The Path Forward

*"The entrepreneur always searches for change, responds to it, and exploits it as an opportunity."*

*Peter Drucker*

We are at a key acceleration point. The imperatives of change are too compelling, too immediate.

Organizations cannot dismiss the need to act. They risk losing valuable talent, ideas, and ultimately customers. At the same time, the path for adoption of new processes, technology, and capabilities to create and deliver a truly differentiated workplace is rich with options detailed in the preceding pages.

Individuals find themselves today with an unprecedented opportunity to influence a workplace that is conducive to their professional, social, and community requirements. Organizations have never had as many participants in an ecosystem that is innovating ever new offerings for the workplace. From organizations dedicated to creating new physical designs of workplaces, and those exploiting niche opportunities to introduce revolutionary digital concepts; from investments in clean, green materials, to smart building solutions; and from those that are reinventing amenities to those that are bringing health into the workplace like never before, it is for decision makers to grab the opportunity, tailor it to their specific needs, and win in their marketplaces (see Figure P4.1).

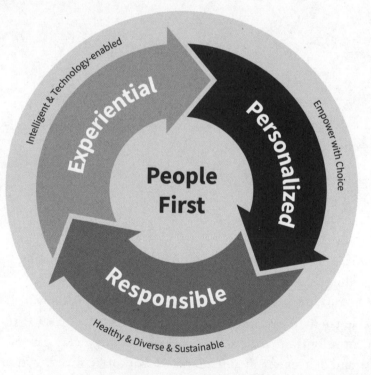

**Figure P4.1   The Path Forward**
**Today's employees prefer workplaces that are**
**experiential, responsible, and personalized.**

The workplace you need *now* requires action – a series of deliberate decisions and prioritization of available and emerging options. In a time of constrained resources, organizations will need to make strategic investments to address the particular needs of workforce and business. Workplace strategies need to be clear and thoughtfully executed.

This will require organizations to grasp the evolution of the traditional view of corporate real estate (CRE), and to think through their own particular strategic positioning, and prioritize the levers of transformation for investment, that lend themselves to create the highest impact.

# 9 | Reimagining the Workplace: How?

*"Revolutions are chaotic."*
*Nicholas Bloom, PhD, Department of Economics, Stanford University*

For real estate and workplace teams, the mandate to shape the future of work has never been stronger. Trends that would have taken years to mature – including digital transformation, hybrid working, and workplace as a talent strategy – were accelerated by the pandemic to become the new standard. In the golden age of the worker, real estate has risen to the top of C-suite priorities for shaping the future of work.

Many companies ramped up and accelerated their digital transformation initiatives as they quickly pivoted to remote working. Now, leading companies recognize that both the pre-pandemic workplace and the forced pandemic remote workplace have benefits and challenges, and lessons to be learned. Continuous adaptation to new and changing conditions will be essential for success. Those that are bold, thoughtful, and timely in reimagining the future stand to gain significant competitive advantage.

For most, the enterprise of the future will involve a digitally enabled, hybrid workplace ecosystem, combining the wide range of work, collaboration, learning, and company-building activities spanning across the office and workspaces elsewhere in an elastic portfolio that can be expanded, adjusted, or optimized as needed. The big winners will be socially responsible companies that lean into workforce preferences, while enabling work, the workforce, and the workplace.

Four strategic priorities have emerged to shape the future of work among companies globally (see Figure 9.1). "People strategy" will be needed to deliver memorable experiences for employees wherever they are working. Business strategy must reimagine work for today's new normal and enterprise talent objectives. Workplace strategy means redefining and redesigning workspaces to support the future of work. Corporate real estate (CRE) strategies will reposition the real estate portfolio to optimize operations and enhance financial performance.[i]

Now, companies will need to decode the new purpose of the office – its function and potential value to employees and to the enterprise. Leading companies are already investing in workplace technologies that help them to better understand how their spaces are being utilized, and creating workplace strategies that ensure continuity between in-office and remote work. They're considering how to retain, recruit, and engage valuable talent in the hybrid work environment, and create more resilient and agile real estate portfolios for the next disruption, wherever it may come from.

At this unique acceleration point, workplace leaders have a powerful opportunity to advance the strategies of the larger enterprise. However, addressing the mandates of business agility, talent engagement, productivity, and efficiency will challenge workplace managers as never before. As organizations adopt work policies, new downsides or benefits may emerge. Not every company is going to get

Figure 9.1   Integrated Enterprise Transformation Model
Four strategic priorities have emerged to shape the
future of work among companies globally.

it right immediately, and it may be difficult to balance the needs of the organization. JLL survey data over the past year has also demonstrated that employees and companies don't yet know exactly what they want. The pandemic was a shock to the system for many, and preferences shaped during a crisis often change or fade when the crisis passes. Companies should be quick to act, but also not overreact. As the saying goes, measure twice and cut once.

From its traditional focus on occupancy costs and hard real estate assets, the CRE function has been transformed into workplace experience management. Among progressive companies, the real estate team has become integrated with HR, finance, and IT teams charged with delivering safe, seamless, and enjoyable experiences across the workplace ecosystem. New skills and capabilities will be needed to advance innovative workplace strategies, prioritize workplace investments, and redefine the corporate real estate portfolio.

The transition to the long-term hybrid working model is not going to be simple, but companies need thoughtful strategies now – or risk losing valuable talent that wants the assurance of flexibility. Missteps will be costly. Some employees will undoubtedly be unhappy with the arrangements their companies offer and will leave for competitors, warns Nicholas Bloom, an economist in Stanford University's Graduate School of Business and one of very few economists who was studying remote work before 2020, when only about 8 percent of Americans were working remotely.[ii]

## The Emerging Winning Model for Workplace

Over the past decade, leading companies began to evaluate their CRE teams not only for how well they could control occupancy costs and keep the lights on, but on how well their workplaces and real estate were actually aligned with, and could even drive, the strategies of the larger business. The pandemic experience demonstrated that remote working could benefit employees and organizations alike – but it also showed that remote working alone is not the answer. Organizations face an urgent need to redefine the meaning and purpose of the workplace. Workplace teams may well be judged for their ability to achieve a triple win for employees, customers, and the enterprise.

Employees win when they gain flexibility and choice, and when their workplaces empower them to achieve professional and personal ambitions. The majority of high-performing employees – 96 percent – are highly satisfied with their workplaces, suggesting a connection between the workplace experience and performance. Winning means having confidence that their workspace – wherever it may be – will provide them with a safe, productive, and enjoyable experience. Providing employees with greater work-life flexibility contributes to higher productivity, engagement, and satisfaction.[iii]

Customers win when the employees who support them are engaged and inspired by their company's culture and purpose. They're more likely to go the extra mile for clients or customers, improving customer satisfaction and overall business performance. Studying public company earnings from 2011 to 2013 and 2014 to 2015, Gallup found that public companies receiving the Gallup Great Workplace Award grew earnings per share by 115 percent, while non-winners grew earnings per share by only 27 percent in the same time period.[iv]

For your organization as a whole, providing personalized, responsible, and experiential workplaces designed for hybrid working can benefit the real estate portfolio, too. While most organizations are adopting hybrid work to support talent and performance strategies, they have the potential to shape a more cost-efficient and purpose-driven real estate footprint that offers the right kinds of facilities and workplaces in the right locations, creating a significant win for the bottom line.

In the new world of dynamic business change and hybrid working, workplace strategy has become a collaborative executive management leadership effort. More than ever, the entire C-suite should be engaged in establishing and implementing a workplace vision aligned with the flexible, dynamic nature of work and one that enables business growth. Chief human resource officers (CHROs) are charged with ensuring that the workplace supports talent and workforce strategies, while CIOs must support the technology investment requirements to fully enable the digital workplace.

## New Workplace Priorities

As work has become at least partially decoupled from a physical space, the corporate office is naturally evolving from a productivity zone into a space for learning and solving complex problems with colleagues – a higher and more valuable purpose than simply being a place to work. For some time, the "workplace" has been morphing into an ecosystem of workspaces – the home office, a coffee shop, an airport lounge, a client site, virtual reality collaboration platforms – rather than a single fixed office.

Organizations have now evolved to fully embrace the ecosystem concept, and many companies have a mandate to create new and diverse, innovative workplace ecosystems comprising digital and physical workspaces designed to meet the evolving expectations of today's talent. In real time, organizations have learned more about which roles can be performed productively in a remote setting and which roles tend to suffer from the lack of proximity, collaboration, and culture. For some employees, flexibility and the option to work remotely will be important factors in how they select jobs in the future. For others, the possibility of dynamic and experiential physical workplaces will be the critical "perk" that leads to engagement and loyalty. Mapping roles and personas to the workplace ecosystem in a way that balances desired outcomes for all will be the great opportunity and challenge ahead.

> "People want to have some control over their time to do what they enjoy. What companies want, in general: get the work done, have good team spirit, alignment of company's goals throughout the ranks," says Rajeev Chaba, president and managing director, MG Motor India, the Indian subsidiary of Chinese automotive manufacturer SAIC Motor. "Companies could try to merge the two – the people and company requirements. But 100 percent from the office or 100 percent from home will not be viable or productive, and the solution lies somewhere in the middle or hybrid model. The companies would try to provide good flexibility in working hours and days and place. The employees may get to choose when to come to office and when to operate from home or some other location. For some jobs, you don't have to be in the office location sometimes and can operate from a holiday home or getaway location. So, what would the office look like? Smaller in size, in multiple locations, maybe a share space concept with short-term leases. The office design would focus more on collaborative spaces, shared spaces, lively atmosphere, space for team building exercises – good cafeteria food, good meeting rooms, and so on. If, in normal times, I had to go for an office space for 100 people, in this new normal, I would go for 50 people with some more meeting rooms and some common working stations."

So, the office still matters. In fact, in many respects it matters more than ever. The thoughtfully designed office continues to provide the best environment for certain work activities. In particular, 70 percent of employees find the office environment more conducive than working at home for team building, management support, and carrying out complex tasks. Also important are human connections. Following the isolation – for some – of working at home, it's not surprising that 60 percent of employees view the office as a place for social interaction. Nearly half of employees are expecting socialization spaces to boost their experience in the office.[vii]

Global organizations will need to determine where they fall within the continuum of work and workplace models, which stretch from almost everyone working in the office almost all the time to everyone working elsewhere most of the time. Determining the model that is best for your company and culture means leaning into employee preferences, while bearing in mind the type of work to be done.

Many employees will want to keep the remote work option to some degree into the future. For many, hybrid working – working in the office sometimes and elsewhere sometimes – has become the new normal and the new preferred way of working. Two-thirds of employees expect to be able to work from different locations when the pandemic recedes,[v] typically using cloud technologies. Employees today want greater workplace flexibility. More than 70 percent of employees want a choice of working hours and flexible schedules, and 57 percent want a choice of workspaces suited to their tasks.[vi]

The challenge, as observed by organizational theorist Lynda Gratton, is to create a hybrid model that considers different roles from the axes of time and place to optimize performance. That is, does a particular role require the synchronous presence of other roles? Does the role work best if everyone is in one place? A team manager, for instance, needs to work at the same time as other team members to provide instant feedback, share ideas, and mentor newer associates. The "place" could be a digital platform like Zoom or Slack, or it could be the office. The key consideration is that the time period in which the team works is more important than the place.[viii]

Be mindful that, no matter what decision framework is used, managers and employees may not agree on the right amount of remote working. Also, the least-experienced workers are more likely to want to be in the office more often, valuing training and meeting with managers, or being more productive in the office.[ix]

Obviously, the right level of remote work flexibility is going to vary from company to company. However, few will pursue all-or-nothing practices. Bloom's conversations with hundreds of managers across different industries points to three days a week as the emerging standard. By spring 2021, companies like Salesforce, Facebook, and HSBC had already announced three-two plans in which employees spend three days in the office and two days at home – along the lines of Monday, Tuesday, and Thursday at the office, Wednesday and Friday at home.[x]

Following a joint Stanford–Nottingham University study of 5,000 UK employees, Bloom concluded that employees prefer the three-days-per-week pattern as well. In fact, employees were willing to give up approximately 6 percent of their wages in exchange for staying home two days per week.[xi]

Other companies have shifted to more office centric plans. Google announced plans to allow employees to work in a hybrid model and is considering other modes of flexibility, all requiring manager approvals and that employees live within commuting distance of a Google office location. As we have discussed elsewhere, Google has long understood the critical value of bringing its talent together physically. Many other companies, especially those blue-chip technology, finance, and banking companies that dominate office occupancy in many markets, are also increasingly encouraging employees to work in the office most of the time.

Diversity, equity, and inclusion (DEI) will matter more than ever. In Bloom's view, companies should offer a uniform schedule for all office employees to establish a clear play field. Otherwise, the years ahead could remain filled with uncertainty and destructive employee turnover. Lack of attention to DEI could lead to policies that inadvertently favor single workers over the working mothers most responsible for the care of small children. Policies also could fail to provide alternative forms of flexibility for workers in frontline jobs that can't be performed at home. Missteps could lead to costly exposure to class-action discrimination lawsuits.[xii]

Workplace strategy should reflect an organization's brand, culture, how teams collaborate and innovate, and should support employee health and wellbeing. In the hybrid environment, an organization must be intentional about culture so it can be incorporated into new ways of working. For example, if a company claims to have a culture built on communication and trust, but limits flexible work options, employees will see the contradiction and believe what they experience over what they are told.

If bringing people together for face-to-face meetings is important, then provide magnet spaces where group meetings can happen. For nearly 90 percent of employees, the office is important for collaborating with team members and building relationships – although that does not necessarily mean they need to be in the office every day.[xiii]

If the culture supports people choosing their in-office days, business leadership should consider hosting activities such as food trucks or a work-life balance coaching session to motivate people to show up at the beginning and end of the week, when utilization tends to drop. Planning for this drop and creating new activities will maximize usage and improve office space ROI. On low-utilization days, an organization could consider using space for community events, coworking, training, health and wellness activities, or other alternative uses.

Informed by organizational culture, a hybrid work strategy begins with understanding who *wants* to work in the office, versus elsewhere. Conversations and surveys also will uncover those who actually *need* to work in the office because they have lively families at home, or lack reliable broadband or a space for an effective home office. For some, the office is a respite from distractions of household activity.

A third group comprises those who *should* work in the office because they are critical to an organization's operations or success.

Roles best performed in the office include, for example, analysts accessing sensitive information or using high-powered computing resources, technical researchers, or product designers using specialized equipment.

Preferences can change over time, so it's important to survey employees periodically. It would be helpful to supplement surveys with benchmarks or audits to track actual behavior, not just what people say they will do. Savvy organizations are implementing a leading human resource (HR) practice of using focus groups or other employee sensing methods once or even twice per month to learn whether their workplace programs are truly meeting employees' needs.

Coming up with the right work model means striking a balance between what works for the organization and what employees want (see Figure 9.2). The CEO may want to see everyone in the office daily, but employees may have other ideas. If other companies in the market offer better options, either more flexibility or better physical workplace experiences, employees will vote with their feet.

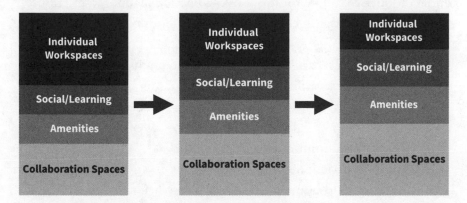

**Figure 9.2 Future of Work: Continuum of Workspace Allocations**
**Workplace allocations may range from traditional to hybrid, depending on an organization's needs and employee preferences, and may evolve over time.**

## What Is Your Human Experience Strategy?

Future-fit and responsible enterprises will reinvent the role their offices play in fostering collaboration and productivity, with human experience at the center. One key initiative will be to develop a human experience strategy, including a change management program, to drive the workplace transformation.

As discussed elsewhere in this book, a people-centric workplace is one that can be personalized for the individual workplace "consumer"; demonstrates social responsibility and environmental sustainability; and provides an engaging, productive experience supported by workplace technologies to streamline daily activities.

On the other side of an anxiety-producing pandemic, prioritizing health and wellbeing – including mental wellbeing – is a given. That's why some companies are adding supportive policies, such as mental health resources, to their total workplace experience. The flexibility of hybrid working inherently addresses the long-lasting effects of the pandemic, providing human connections for those who felt isolated and a productive respite for those overwhelmed by competing household demands. For all, a choice of workspace options is empowering, providing a liberating sense of control.

While the office can't address every issue, what an organization can do is provide a variety of spaces for different activities, whether working solo, collaborating with a group, or socializing over a cup of coffee. Plants, natural light, outdoor spaces – all offer a respite from daily stress and can inspire creative thinking.

Providing a variety of workspace options, in and out of the office, is a critical aspect of a people-centric workplace strategy. Inside the office, there may be a need to make workplace investments to provide the right spaces for different kinds of work. Employees are willing to accept trade-offs – 67 percent of employees would adopt a "hot-desk" environment of shared individual workspaces in exchange for more diverse office spaces and flexible work-from-home policies. In particular, employees say that spaces dedicated to heads-down, focused work are second only to socialization spaces among options that would significantly boost the office experience.[xiv]

Technology is the key enabler to ensure that employees benefit from a holistic high-quality experience across the workplace ecosystem. Innovations such as people analytics solutions, artificial intelligence assistants, and workflow management tools have the potential to streamline traditional workplace procedures and create new opportunities to empower employees to personalize their work experience.[xv] Collaboration between the workplace, real estate, and information technology departments is essential to provide employees with access to the data and applications they need wherever they are working, to ensure continuity and fluidity between in-office and remote work.

For example, those who work mostly at home may need help optimizing their home internet routers, or company-paid investments in higher-capacity broadband connections. Home is now another workplace that the organization is provisioning, and workers may need other essentials for high performance, such as laptops, second monitors, and ergonomic chairs. Not everyone will have the same resources, so remote work policies should define specific technology requirements for all employees working outside the office to support productivity and a sense of belonging. Security policies and tools are important, too. A household of multiple people working remotely on any given day could potentially put confidential information or company networks at risk.[xvi]

Fortuitously, many companies began migrating to cloud services years before the pandemic, streamlining access to office resources. Platforms like Microsoft's Office and Google Workspace (formerly G-Suite) enabled office workers to connect with office software and data on demand when many offices closed during the pandemic.

Cloud service adoption was a harbinger of increased remote work. "We are moving towards an era in which technology becomes commoditized in a 'bring your own' agnostic ecosystem," says Philip Ross, founder and CEO of UnWork, a management consultancy and research firm focused on the future of work. "The benefits of mobility and choice will become recognized in a peripatetic workplace where people are free to choose. But imperfect information needs to be corrected by new workplace technology that builds on data, machine learning and AI to shape how work gets done."

Seamless workplace collaboration is the goal, whether an employee is working from the office or from the remote workplace or home work environment. These days, most companies have turned to Microsoft Teams, Dropbox, Google Meet, Zoom, and Slack for virtual meetings and collaboration, and these tools will undoubtedly become increasingly feature-rich over time. In the hybrid workplace, collaboration between, for example, a team in a conference room and team members off-site will be increasingly common.

Inside the office, workplace experience leaders have the power to make the workday easier by providing such tools as mobile experience apps and automated work order management tools that enable fast response to facility management work orders. Employees are happier when the leaky toilet in the bathroom is fixed quickly or when they can place lunch orders for a last-minute meeting via an app. Using a mobile app to reserve a workspace or conference room, or easily locate and connect with a colleague to collaborate, goes a long way toward reducing frustration and boosting employee satisfaction.

Enabling a digital workplace won't happen overnight and may involve investments in new technologies. To create an effective roadmap for the technology-enabled workplace you envision, it's important to tap the right talent and partners to navigate the growing universe of *proptech* – property technology – innovations.

## Prioritizing Workplace Investments

Implementing a hybrid workplace strategy will likely involve workplace investments. Leading companies are already investing in workplace technologies that help them to better understand how their spaces are being utilized to inform investment decisions. Whereas 30–40 percent of today's offices comprise collaborative and social spaces, those spaces could comprise 50–70 percent of the future office, with 30–50 percent dedicated to individual workspaces, amenities, and social and learning spaces.[xvii]

Thoughtful planning will help determine how many and what types of workspaces the office actually needs. Clearly, the traditional one-person-to-one-desk ratio isn't relevant in the hybrid working model – people who plan to be in the office only a few days a week may not need dedicated offices or assigned desks. Instead, workplace utilization or density should be based on the ratio of people to seats available – and the headcount will vary from day to day or even hour to hour. Creative layouts will enable organizations to expand headcount without necessarily expanding footprint costs.

Bearing in mind that social distancing may continue to be valuable, workplace utilization should aim to optimize occupancy on any given day as headcounts wax and wane. Overcrowding creates an uncomfortable, less productive experience, while underutilization means wasted space and budget with fewer opportunities for chance encounters. Employee and company research suggests that at least some "de-densification" of seating plans, with more space allocated per person, could offset some of the lower utilization expected on any given day.

When the CFO begins questioning the cost of creating a great workplace experience, nothing is more persuasive than a strong business case. Real estate can be costly – but the cost and value of talent is greater. Focusing on desired performance outcomes is becoming the new approach to prioritizing investments. For example, investments in digital tools that show who will be in the office at the same time will further enable valuable face-to-face connections at work. Investments in modular, movable office furniture would create an agile office, able to support brainstorming, a stand-up meeting, or a training workshop in a single space.[xviii]

Designing for mobile and hybrid work creates office trade-offs, usually in the form of fewer dedicated personal desks and more shared resources and amenities. Often, reducing the number of personal desks in the office can free up funds for the workplace investment. That's another reason for smart planning – it literally pays off.

Also, some companies have found pockets of opportunity to fund office upgrades by negotiating with landlords eager to sign longer leases. If a particular location fits needed talent and experience strategies, organizations may have an opportune moment to renegotiate the lease and direct the savings to creating more collaboration spaces or providing ergonomic desks or upgraded Wi-Fi connections for employees who work at home.

For building owners and landlords, this shake-up also presents a great opportunity and challenge to ensure that assets are attractive for today's corporate tenants. Buildings in accessible, amenities-rich locations, with robust digital infrastructure and energy-efficient operating systems, will outperform those less responsive to employee expectations. Creating and operating great workplaces will inevitably become a partnership between landlords, high-quality real estate partners, tenants, and their employees. The need for talent and high-performance workplaces is shifting CRE from a simple business-to-business model to a more complex and valuable business-to-business-to-consumer dynamic.

## Managing the Dynamic Hybrid Workplace and Optimizing the Real Estate Portfolio

If companies learned one thing during the pandemic, it was how to be flexible. In the postpandemic era, businesses will need agile strategies to pivot, expand, or shrink their footprints in response to changing business conditions and employees' work preferences. In a world of disruptions and changing attitudes and behaviors, the key to resiliency is elasticity: a CRE portfolio that can easily shrink or expand.

In hybrid office models, elastic real estate strategies can accommodate today's distributed workforces that may include full-time employees and on-demand talent. Many companies are building in elasticity with flexible spaces, coworking facilities, short-term lease agreements, or on-demand structures that can be ramped up or down as needs and headcount change. Mergers, dispositions, restructurings, and rapid growth will be business-as-usual, and the real estate portfolio will need to adjust seamlessly to these enterprise challenges.

When leaders and teams need to come together, for instance, a collaboration space run by a third party, such as a coworking space or hotel conference room, might be more convenient and also more productive because of fewer day-to-day office distractions. If suburban employees don't want to commute to the CBD, but need office space for project collaboration, a smaller headquarters office and more flexible suburban options might be the answer.

As much as 31 percent of corporate portfolios may comprise short-term or on-demand flexible spaces rather than space that is owned or locked into long-term leases.[xix] In fact, the pandemic increased flexible space demand that was already growing. Now, 67 percent of decision-makers are increasing workplace mobility programs and incorporating flexible space as a central element of their agile work strategies. In a time of economic uncertainty, flexible space solutions can support portfolio reductions and cost-saving strategies. In the longer term, a portfolio mix of traditional and flexible spaces will be even more important to meet employee demands for shorter commutes and less-dense workplaces that prioritize health and wellbeing.[xx]

In this environment, portfolio optimization – including "smart"-sizing and restacking space – becomes an always-on activity rather than an occasional project. The CRE portfolio is no longer a slow-moving container ship, but more like a fleet of agile sailboats. Building on the win-win-win approach to workplace and real estate portfolio space optimization as an overarching goal, effective space utilization, and optimizing the office space portfolio to match evolving stakeholder needs are going to be important.

## Identifying Experience Metrics That Matter

The traditional measures of cost savings, operating costs, and cost per square foot can be helpful, but don't reflect the extent to which the workplace is addressing employee preferences, improving talent retention and supporting business strategies. The hybrid people-centric workplace is going to require different kinds of workplace performance metrics – and the days of "set it and forget it" workplace strategy are long gone.

Instead, organizations will need tools for ongoing monitoring and measurement, along with continual adjustments as employee needs evolve. Given the high value of talent, metrics should focus on employee satisfaction, engagement, and experience rather than on real estate costs alone. Consider what is most important to employees and what additional experience measures would make sense for measuring workplace effectiveness in the office. For example, comparing turnover or sick days at different facilities, for instance, can reveal which locations are better for health, wellness, and productivity than others.

Also, new platforms and methodologies are becoming available to help measure aspects of the office experience. By combining surveys and human experience analytics, organizations can uncover insights into how employee perceptions of their workplaces – including their own home offices – are supporting productivity, collaboration, well-being, work-life balance, and more.

It's possible to create a framework for measuring how well an office and its culture support talent attraction, retention, productivity, and engagement. By blending research on a company's workplace mobility programs, green building design, social networks, location, and employee services, leading organizations will uncover which workplace strategies and experience programs matter most in the war for talent and compare their strategy to those of competitors.

## From Corporate Real Estate Team to Workplace Experience Manager

Stepping up to the challenge of the triple-win will require fundamental changes in how CRE is managed: what got us where we are today will not get us where we need to go tomorrow. Navigating the journey to the agile, yet also personalized, responsible, and experiential, hybrid workplace ecosystem will require new leadership skills for driving the workplace conversation.

### Collaboration Skills

The hybrid workplace won't be created in a vacuum, but should reflect organizational goals, talent strategies, policies, and practices. For that reason, workplace leaders will need to be collaborators with their C-suite colleagues. CFOs will still be focused on real estate efficiency and cost, but the CFO is only one stakeholder of many in the people-centric hybrid workplace model. Ideally, workplace strategy will be aligned with the CEO's business strategies and HR's talent strategies. The CIO will be a key partner for enabling the digital workplace, while the chief sustainability officer will be a collaborator for facilities-related sustainability initiatives.

Finance still matters, of course, to fund workplace investments and leverage the cost savings of portfolio optimization, but partnership and communication with the CIO is important to demonstrate the enterprise value of the workplace. If reallocated space is viewed simply as a portfolio reduction or real estate investment, the workplace team's contributions to talent recruitment and retention, employee engagement, and business performance will be easily overlooked. Updating space use may require substantial investments in talent and technology that, ultimately, will benefit the entire enterprise. Engaging other C-suite leaders will help reposition the CRE team from being purely transactional to being the driver of a holistic workplace business case.

Since workplace strategies are a collaborative effort, soft "people skills" are becoming an important CRE leadership characteristic. Managing the portfolio is becoming increasingly dynamic, which means CRE teams will need to be able to manage large complex teams and relationships. With the ability to forge alliances across the organization, the CRE team will be better equipped to anticipate business requirements and pivot as situations require.

An integrated approach to hybrid work styles and an optimized real estate portfolio is helping utility companies boost productivity and retain call-center staff. During the pandemic, one utility's real estate, HR, and IT teams jointly decided to close local call-center facilities and sent staff home to work remotely – and safely. The companies found that remote work didn't affect productivity for these roles. In fact, call-center staff retention improved because staff didn't have to commute to offices that were hard to reach using public transportation – a situation that had led to high levels of attrition in the past. Attrition at one call center dropped from 50 percent to 20 percent because of remote work implemented at the start of the pandemic.

Another important soft skill is the ability to manage change. Proactively managing change reduces the *disruption dip* that change invariably produces. Since change will likely be ongoing, the CRE team will need to be able to develop and deliver global messaging and communications strategies and proactively engage with leaders across the organization.

## Operations and Business Acumen

Managing "always on" workplace change and portfolio optimization is going to demand greater operational skills from CRE leaders, and more business acumen. As CRE evolves from a static utility to a force for employee performance, CRE teams will need to adopt the mindset of business transformation to reimagine the workplace and orchestrate its redefinition.

## Data-Driven Decision-Making

Advances in AI and machine learning, robotics, automation, the Internet of Things, and cloud computing have brought digital transformation to nearly every aspect of CRE management. Many facility management, building and workplace technologies are now available, with powerful capabilities for streamlining workplace management, managing workplace utilization, and nearly every other aspect of CRE management.

Today's building technologies – from electronic security badges and wireless sensors to smart building systems and intelligent lighting – generate voluminous data about how and when employees are using their corporate workplaces. These systems enable building engineers to fine-tune building efficiency and workplace managers to adjust office layouts in response to real-world, actual usage. Technologies from companies like VergeSense, for example, gather data on movement of people throughout a space, monitor when a space should be reset or cleaned, analyze how amenities are being used, and even sound the alarm if capacity is exceeded.

These technologies will enable companies and offices to better manage the hybrid workplace.[xxi]

While it is not necessary to be an expert programmer to benefit from data and analytics, a successful team will either build or "buy" expertise in data and analytics to exploit today's new platforms and make data-driven decisions. Understanding the fundamentals of data governance and the possibilities offered by today's analytics platforms has become a critical skill set for CRE executive as data increasingly drives performance.

### *Creating a Culture of Innovation*

Combined with new ways of working, the explosion of building and workplace technologies provides fertile ground for cultivating new ideas for the workplace experience. However, wholesale adoption of unproven concepts or tools poses risk. What if a new layout is unpopular? What if employees or the workplace team fail to embrace what was supposed to be a valuable new technology tool?

Often, testing with a prototype or pilot program offers the less risky approach. A new layout or furniture configuration can be tested with a limited number of workgroups and modified in response to sensor data and employee feedback. Similarly, new technology can be piloted with a limited group.

Some leading companies have established teams focused on workplace innovation or on workplace technologies specifically. These teams investigate emerging and maturing concepts and technologies that may warrant a pilot program, helping the workplace team keep pace with larger business change. Employees are likely experimenting regularly with new technologies at home – and they expect their companies to be experimenting, too.

### The Challenge of Workplace Transformation

Achieving the triple win of workplace transformation for the organization, employees, and customers means change across multiple dimensions. Once a static, periodic project, now workplace strategy must become a dynamic response to evolving employee wants, needs, and expectations in the golden age of the worker. The new CRE portfolio strategy is always-on optimization. Creating and managing the workplace ecosystem – beyond the fixed workplace – is no longer the domain of the CRE team alone, but must become a collaboration between CRE, IT, HR, and finance to advance the organization's business goals and talent strategies.

Above all, the human experience in the workplace has come to the forefront as a driver of organizational success, creating new demands for CRE teams. A new mindset and new skills are essential to rise to the challenge of the hybrid workplace model and the future of work.

## SOURCES CITED

i. "Shaping the future of work for a better world," JLL Research, January 2021, https://www.us.jll.com/en/trends-and-insights/research/reimagine-the-new-future-of-work-to-shape-a-better-world.

ii. Aka Ito, "America's Best Work-From-Home Expert Is Bracing for Turmoil," *Business Insider,* April 13, 2021, https://www.businessinsider.com/wfh-expert-economist-nick-bloom-says-future-of-work-messy-2021-4?r=rr.

iii. Flore Pradère, "From Productivity to Human Performance," JLL Research, October 2020, https://www.us.jll.com/en/trends-and-insights/research/from-productivity-to-human-performance.

iv. Ed O'Boyle, "State of the American Workplace," Gallup, 2017, https://www.gallup.com/workplace/238085/state-american-workplace-report-2017.aspx.

v. Edward Connolly and Michael Billing, "What the Hybrid Workplace Means for Real Estate," JLL, 2021, https://www.us.jll.com/en/views/what-the-hybrid-workplace-means-for-real-estate.

vi. "Reimagining Human Experience: How to Embrace the New Work-Life Priorities and Expectations of a Liquid Workforce," JLL Research, November 2020, https://www.us.jll.com/en/trends-and-insights/research/global-work force-expectations-shifting-due-to-covid-19.

vii. "Reimagine: The New Future of Work to Shape a Better World," JLL Research, 2021, https://www.us.jll.com/en/trends-and-insights/research/reimagine-the-new-future-of-work-to-shape-a-better-world.

viii. Lynda Gratton, "How to Do Hybrid Right," *Harvard Business Review*, May-June 2021, https://hbr.org/2021/05/how-to-do-hybrid-right.

ix. Deniz Caglar, Vinay Couto, Ed Faccio, Bhushan Sethi, "PWC Remote Work Survey," PWC, January 2021, https://www.pwc.com/us/en/library/covid-19/us-remote-work-survey.html.

x. Nicholas Bloom, "Our Research Shows Working from Home Works, in Moderation," *The Guardian,* March 21, 2021, https://www.theguardian.com/commentisfree/2021/mar/21/research-working-from-home.

xi. Ibid.

xii. Ito, "America's Best Work-From-Home Expert Is Bracing for Turmoil."

xiii. Caglar et al. "PWC Remote Work Survey."

xiv. "Reimagining Human Experience: How to Embrace the New Work-Life Priorities and Expectations of a Liquid Workforce," JLL Research, November 2020, https://www.us.jll.com/en/trends-and-insights/research/global-workforce-expectations-shifting-due-to-covid-19.

xv. Owen Hughes, "Future of Work: Five New Features of Your Remote Workplace in 2021," *ZDNet,* December 22, 2020, https://www.zdnet.com/article/future-of-work-five-new-features-of-your-remote-workplace-in-2021/.

xvi. Meghan Rimol, "Four Ways for CIOs to Implement Hybrid Working in 2021," *Smarter with Gartner,* March 2021, https://www.gartner.com/smarterwithgartner/4-ways-for-cios-to-implement-hybrid-working-in-2021/.

xvii. "How to Prepare for the Hybrid Workplace," webinar, JLL Technologies, 2021, https://www.jllt.com/video/how-to-prepare-for-the-hybrid-workplace/thank-you.

xviii. Gerald C. Kane, Rich Nanda, Anh Phillips, and Jonathan Copulsky, "Redesigning the Post-Pandemic Workplace," *MIT Sloan Management Review,* February 10, 2021, https://sloanreview.mit.edu/article/redesigning-the-post-pandemic-workplace/.

xix. The Impact of COVID-19 on Flexible Space," JLL Research, July 2020, https://www.us.jll.com/en/trends-and-insights/research/the-impact-of-covid19-on-flexible-space.

xx. "Beyond Re-entry: An Occupier Journey to the Next Normal," JLL Research, September 15, 2020, https://www.us.jll.com/en/trends-and-insights/research/reimagine-for-occupiers.

xxi. Yishai Lerner, "JLL Thinking Inside the Box When It Comes to the New Office Normal," *Real Estate Weekly,* March 5, 2021, https://rew-online.com/jll-thinking-inside-the-box-when-it-comes-to-new-office-normal/.

# 10 | Strategic Framework: Journey to the Hybrid Workplace

*"Every great dream begins with a dreamer. Always remember, you have within you the strength, the patience, and the passion to reach for the stars to change the world."*

*Harriet Tubman, Abolitionist, Political Activist*

So where to go from here? For many companies, the status quo is clearly not an option. In a hypercompetitive, globalized world, every organization needs to leverage the power of an effective workplace more than ever before in order to win the war for talent. The desires of individuals and organizations alike for workplace transformation are compelling and overwhelming. Demands for personalization, the distinct preferences of multiple generations in the workforce, the growing expectations for purposeful, responsible workplaces, the opportunities that intelligent, immersive, and experiential workplaces can create – all are converging to create an undeniable imperative.

As discussed elsewhere in this book, the extremes of complete working from home and the pre-2020 model of mostly working in the office create a spectrum with advantages and challenges. As organizations consider a framework for decision-making, revisiting the various dimensions of transformation will help inform their strategy.

## 1.0 Elements of The Personalized Workplace

Given the availability of personalized and configurable experiences in the consumer realm, today's multigenerational and often fluid workforce has growing expectations for personalized workplace experiences as well. Functional, vibrant settings – tailored to employee preferences, providing workspace options, and enabled by technology – will transform the office into a beacon for talent.

### *Workplace Ecosystem*

Personalization begins with the hybrid ecosystem of workplaces, giving employees the latitude to work in the office some of the time and elsewhere at other times. Providing activity-based workspaces within the office or convenient off-site flexible workplaces empowers employees to choose the right kind of workspace for the work to be performed. Space must become adaptable and easily configured to provide the right mix of individual and group spaces for solo work, collaboration, learning, creativity, and socializing. Optimizing your workplaces becomes less about achieving high density and more about providing places that will attract, retain, and engage talent.

The adaptability and configurability of space, complete with the use of modular designs and an enhanced focus on optimal combination of individual and communal spaces, albeit defying the drive of recent times to densify spaces, provides organizations with unique opportunities to engage, attract, and retain talent.

## *Agile Real Estate Portfolio*

Personalization means tailoring the workplace ecosystem to the needs and preferences of employees, with an agile real estate portfolio that can evolve to match supply and demand for workspaces. Options might include not only the office or an employee's home, but also a coworking space, a small satellite office for employees who live in the suburbs, or a short-term leased space for a specific project team.

## *Digital Technologies*

Digital technologies are essential for enabling the personalized workplace and seamlessly blending the physical and virtual worlds. Those working remotely will need to be equipped with access to high-speed internet and company resources. In the office, workplace mobile apps and smart building technologies will streamline everyday tasks, from reserving workspaces and locating colleagues to exploring on-site amenities. Today's data-driven workplace management and scheduling tools can drive planning to ensure that teams are in the office to collaborate together – and that everyone has the workspaces they need for the day.

As is increasingly evident, the drive toward personalization is becoming pervasive. As an impetus for workplace transformation, personalization done well is an investment in creating value from an organization's people and places.

## 2.0 Elements of the Responsible Workplace

Against the backdrop of public dialogue about health, inequality and social justice, climate change, and environmental sustainability, corporate social responsibility has become a factor in talent recruitment and retention. A responsible workplace addresses contemporary concerns by demonstrating genuine, visible care and concern for employees and the larger world.

## Health and Wellbeing

The value of health and wellbeing features in the office has long been recognized in thoughtful office design – but never more than now, on the heels of the global pandemic. Air quality, water quality, nutrition and fitness, touchless technologies, and sanitizing regimens are front and center for organizations focused on revitalizing their offices. Employees may enjoy the human connections to be found in the office, but remain keenly aware of health risks. Following the stress and anxiety that accompanies a global health crisis, mental health has come to the forefront as well.

While very stressful for some, a year away from the office led others to spend more time outdoors and increase their focus on wellness. Thoughtful health and wellness programming can provide "sips" of health and wellness throughout the office with outdoor spaces, green walls of plants, on-site yoga or meditation spaces, nutrition and health resources, and other features that support wellbeing. Depending on employee preferences, on-site fitness amenities or access to a nearby gym may also convey to employees that their health and wellness is important.

## Environmental Sustainability

Although climate change and environmental sustainability are subject to a spectrum of opinions, the issues are important to the younger generations of workers – and to many other stakeholders. In addition, the economic and health benefits of smart and digitized, yet energy-efficient, workplaces and facilities constitute a call to action.

New building technologies and renewable energy solutions are available to create more sustainable facilities, and high-efficiency smart building systems add to the employee experience by improving indoor air quality. Energy retrofits, "greening" the facilities supply chain, recycling programs, and data-driven predictive maintenance are among the many options available for bringing environmental sustainability to the office in an apolitical manner.

Many leading organizations have made public commitments to net-zero carbon emissions goals as a rallying call for action. Yet, many struggle to develop a strategy and a reliable plan to achieve their ambitions. Since buildings account for approximately 40 percent of the world's greenhouse gas emissions, real estate and workplace teams are often on the frontlines of helping meet emissions targets and creating a holistic approach to deliver on social and economic advantages of a responsible workplace.

New facilities and workplace technologies are available to support facilities goals. Leading workplace and facility management teams already use IoT devices for data-driven space management. Smart building systems connected by IoT devices self-adjust in response to occupancy and environmental conditions to fine-tune air quality and temperature, reducing energy waste.

One company, Invicara, has developed technology that creates a visual digital twin of a building – down to every piece of building equipment – that can be used to pilot facilities management technologies and analyze detailed performance data to drive adoption of innovative solutions while avoiding costly missteps. Microsoft uses digital twins to manage a portion of its large Redmond, Washington, headquarters campus, modeling physical spaces with real-time data indicating where and when people are using the facilities.

### *Diversity, Equity, and Inclusion*

The responsible workplace also addresses diversity, equity, and inclusion (DEI). While the drive to create workplaces that are safe, nurturing, and supportive of individuals of diverse backgrounds is not entirely new, 2020's surge in social justice activism has sparked a sense of urgency. Many leading organizations have committed to becoming more inclusive and equitable – and younger generations of workers are paying attention.

Inside the office, real estate and workplace teams can support DEI through thoughtful policies and initiatives that advance social change. *As discussed in Chapter 5, Microsoft's new campus in Quarry Yards on Atlanta's economically underdeveloped west side will help Microsoft attract a diverse workforce – but it also includes land reserved for retail and health care facilities badly needed in the Quarry Yards community.*

## 3.0 Elements of the Experiential Workplace

From the personalization imperative comes a mandate for a memorable and positive workplace experience. Ideally, the workplace will manifest an organization's unique culture and values, just as retailers intentionally design around the customer's journey from exploration to purchase – whether online or in a physical store.

Steve Brashear is senior vice president, Global Real Estate, at Salesforce, the undisputed global leader in customer relationship management. Salesforce's success is an enviable story of capturing and creating value that has resonated across the globe for over two decades.

Brashear leads Salesforce's Real Estate and Workplace Services team across the globe, including nine Salesforce Towers that have grown and continue to evolve along with the company. "Our offices are physical representations of our culture," says Brashear. He cites a strategy that has differentiated Salesforce workplaces and has been a beacon for its brand from the company's inception. While he agrees wholeheartedly that the workplace is going through a significant transformation, the core elements of Salesforce's culture and experience have not changed because of the pandemic. Location has always been critical, and prime locations in central business districts in most of their locations continue to be at the center of the company's strategy.

"We have prioritized and invested in design that is consistent and standard across all our offices," says Brashear. "This design, known as the Salesforce Design Standard, brings a sense of calmness and belonging to our people, while putting sustainability at the forefront." In Brashear's view, these elements are even more essential today than they have ever been, and "provide a seamless experience globally."

"The definition of the workplace is shifting," says Brashear, "and it's no longer defined by the four walls of an office building. We believe in creating success from anywhere." Salesforce has always had a policy of flexibility, with its employees traveling to various clients and offices, and working from home.

"We have always known how to be productive and successful without being fully in the office. However, people need the human connection," says Brashear. "They need to see their peers. They need to get away from the distractions of home. Social and psychological activity and wellbeing are essential, and the office is the place to achieve that connection and belonging."

Salesforce's Work.com platform enables the company to create a seamless experience for the company, and develop a frictionless, productive day for everyone who comes to the office. And Salesforce is Work.com's "customer zero" – its learnings influence its customers' return to the workplace.

"The bridging of the physical and digital environment is core to creating these experiences," says Brashear. It is how Salesforce is embracing the future of work that is purposeful and inspiring, while staying true to its core values.

Salesforce's spaces are welcoming for employees, customers, families, and visitors alike. Brashear highlights the company's commitment to local communities. "The top floors of our offices are unlike any other. They are communal hospitality spaces, or, as we like to call them, 'Ohana Floors – designed to be open and multifunctional places that promote collaboration. The unparalleled city views are inspiring. These spaces are available for employees during the day and for nonprofits to hold events on evenings and weekends, at no cost."

Done well, workplace experience is a differentiator that creates an invaluable sense of belonging and pride that boosts employee engagement. Viewing the workplace through the lens of "product," workplace strategy should be informed by the preferences and behaviors of the workplace consumers – employees, clients, and other visitors – just as retailers continuously track and analyze customer data to prompt interest, engage, and build loyalty.

Workplace design has evolved to address the need for truly inspirational, functional, and healthy spaces that inspire creativity and foster collaboration. Today's workplace must provide value beyond just providing a space, but by offering an experience that is unavailable elsewhere and meets employees' need for in-person connections, learning, socializing – and an enjoyable, productive workday.

Fundamental to the experience is the workspace itself. Through workplace sensors and IoT devices, forward-looking organizations are using real-time data and analytics to dynamically manage their space allocations. As the hybrid workplace evolves, the ability to rapidly reconfigure layouts to accommodate demand for particular types of workspaces will be invaluable for providing a fulfilling and productive experience. Also critical, agile workplaces enable always-on portfolio optimization that reduces waste while supporting the needs of the workforce.

Intelligent optimization of real estate portfolios is leading to optimization of space requirements and assignment. Dynamically managing and planning occupancy through the targeted use of sensors and AI is allowing for a real-time allocation of space – particularly critical in the hybrid work environments that have emerged.

The workplace experience extends beyond the office, too. Personalization contributes to experience by providing workspace options in and out of the office, along with technologies to support a fulfilling workday. Attending to the employee's need for robust internet access or providing an allowance to fund an ergonomic home office extends the office experience to the home.

The experiential office also includes technology for the intelligent workplace. Digital whiteboards, wayfinding kiosks and mobile apps, intelligent lighting that responds to the availability of natural light – the explosion of property technology – *proptech* – have brought a broad range of possibilities to the workplace. Smart building systems now can be configured to empower employees to control temperature and lighting in their workspaces.

Forward-looking organizations are adopting immersive virtual, augmented, and mixed-reality technologies enabled by AI to bridge the gap between the physical and virtual world. In a virtual reality meeting, for example, two attendees could have a side conversation, or a host avatar could walk through a presentation or demonstration with an audience of employee avatars. Telepresence robots are another possibility, enabling a remote worker to attend a meeting or stop by a colleague's desk from 100 – or 1,000 – miles away.

## Path to Strategic Workplace Decisions

Resources by definition are limited at even the most profitable organizations. Competing priorities demand capital, and every initiative must be backed by a strong business case and return on investment. One size, indeed, does not fit all.

The good news is that real estate and workplaces have gained growing recognition as a source of enterprise value creation. Among progressive organizations, the workplace has become a valuable asset worthy of investment as the nexus of talent, brand, culture, creativity, and innovation, trumping the historical focus purely on occupancy costs.

The old, archaic practices of driving office density, mandatory office "face time," divesting real estate assets without a strategy, or turning off all the lights at 6:00 p.m. regardless of occupancy, have gone by the wayside. Moving forward, every organization will have to consider its path toward a compelling workplace and ecosystem, while employees weigh their desire to work at home against the opportunity to spend time in an appealing, vibrant office. Every organization will need to identify the unique workplace facets it needs and create an intentional strategy around workplace design and management. No answer is necessarily wrong, other than choosing the status quo. At this inflection point from the prepandemic workplace and all that is to follow, embracing workplace transformation is a strategic imperative.

We suggest the following two-step framework for evaluating your unique environments and priorities. Each step will help you ask the right questions to understand how best to allocate resources.

### *Step 1: How Complex Is Your Environment?*

The first step is to assign a value to key drivers of complexity as they pertain to your industry and your company, including industry maturity, competition, stakeholders, geographic presence, talent profile, and organizational strategy. The more complex, dynamic, and competitive your industry, the higher the complexity value will be. Assigning values to each driver will highlight the urgency and magnitude of your workplace needs, and will help provide the basis of a business case for investments and change. If your situation is highly complex, for example, your total value will be 600; in a very simple world, the value could be as low as 60 (see Figure 10.1).

| Complexity Driver | High Value = 100 | Medium Value = 50 | Low Value = 10 | Assigned Value |
|---|---|---|---|---|
| Industry dynamics | Growth-oriented, reliance on rapid process, product, and brand innovation | Established industry and fundamentally stable processes with aspirations to leverage emerging capabilities (e.g., digital) | Highly regulated with limited competition | |
| Competitive landscape | Highly competitive, digitally disrupted, reliant on adjacent ecosystem partners | Multiple smaller competitors targeting parts of the value chain through innovative disruption | Stable oligopoly | |
| Stakeholder profile – employees, customers, stakeholders | Activists that demand progressive actions (e.g., corporate responsibility, net zero actions) | Sensitized and recognizing the need for intervention | Stable with focus on corporate social responsibility adopting a building-block approach | |
| Geographic presence | Global and strategically consistent | Multinational – tailored to regional nuances | Regional, with relatively less proliferation of employee and customer needs | |
| Talent profile | Highly portable and fluid | Undergoing disruption from new generations | Largely stable with tenures | |
| Organizational strategy | Differentiation via product/service innovation | Growth-driven via scale and operational efficiency | Success built from and reliant on existing brand domination | |
| TOTAL VALUE | | | | |

**Figure 10.1 Drivers of Workplace Complexity**

**The more complex, dynamic, and competitive your industry, the higher the complexity value will be.**

Each organization will need to assess its own environments against these and other applicable criteria. A highly competitive industry that relies on rapid product and service innovation for success, for example, will face intense competition for a complex set of skillsets from other companies in many industries. Understanding the complexity drivers and their relative importance to the organization and its stakeholders will help uncover possible workplace strategies, policies, processes, and necessary investments.

A high score approaching 600 is a call to action – the risks of maintaining the status quo may be too high for the organization. A thoughtful, strategic path to workplace transformation may indeed be an imperative. Organizations that score closer to 60 may find that their imperative to act is not as pronounced. These enterprises may have the luxury of a slower path to transformation, with the caveat that, in a hyper-competitive world of competing ecosystems, the idea that any industry or organization is insulated and protected may not stand the test of time.

### *Step 2: What Does Your Workplace Need to Be?*

Step 2 provides an approach for determining your organization's path along the continuum from "fast follower" to "leader." Once again, there are no wrong choices – but prioritizing everything means prioritizing nothing. An attempt to lead across all dimensions creates the risk of diluting the impact on the most critical area. Leaders and innovators tend to commit to a particular facet, taking risks along the way, driven by assessments of their unique context and priorities. The fast follower is measured, adapts, invests, and seeks lessons learned and a risk-mitigation approach to action. Most organizations will have some characteristics of both Fast Followers and Leaders, however (see Figure 10.2).

| Organizational Priorities | From Fast Follower | To Leader |
| --- | --- | --- |
| The Personalized Workplace<br>*Empower with Choice*<br><br>Support flexible, customizable, workplace options tailored to employee preferences. | • Design a workplace program that fits organizational priorities.<br>• Create a robust technology-enabled process for in-office team scheduling.<br>• Deploy activity-based workplace.<br>• Design for adaptable and configurable space. | • Adopt a learning mindset and workplaces that adapt to an evolving environment.<br>• Provide end-to-end workplace experiences aligned with business goals and culture.<br>• Use technology to personalize the workplace experience.<br>• Provide convenient, on-demand space options. |
| The Responsible Workplace<br>*Act with Purpose*<br><br>Create healthy, safe, equitable, and sustainable workplaces for everyone. | • Commit to carbon neutrality and energy efficiency targets.<br>• Invest in retrofitting programs and enhance focus on healthy buildings.<br>• Prioritize sustainability across the supply chain.<br>• Provide an app to support healthy lifestyles in the office.<br>• Improve employee engagement, equality, and inclusion. | • Declare and create a roadmap for net-zero goals and targets.<br>• Harness the benefits of a smart, digitized, and energy-efficient workplace.<br>• Support nutrition plans for employees wherever they work.<br>• Go beyond the workplace to institute programs to advance social change.<br>• Make workplaces safe, nurturing, and supportive of individuals of diverse backgrounds and experiences. |

| Organizational Priorities | From Fast Follower | To Leader |
|---|---|---|
| The Experiential Workplace *Enhance through Experience*<br><br>Create dynamic technology-enabled work environments that inspire human performance. | • Invest in physical and digital experiences in the office.<br>• Institute data and insight-driven analytics.<br>• Implement risk-based predictive maintenance.<br>• Boost access. | • Deliver integrated experiences anywhere work happens.<br>• Redesign space to make the workplace a social hub and destination.<br>• Provide tech-enabled solutions for anywhere, anytime working.<br>• Invest in immersive virtual technologies enabled by AI.<br>• Manage occupancy planning dynamically. |

**Figure 10.2 From Fast Follower to Leader**
**Leaders and innovators excel at adapting as circumstances evolve, learning from feedback from employees and from organizational performance.**

While uncertainty is bound to bring some trepidation to decision-making, a wide spectrum of organizations has already seized the opportunity for change and is already benefiting from workplace transformations. They've worked to overcome the trauma of the pandemic, along with its isolating and stress-inducing effects, to provide environments that support the tangible and psychological needs of their talent.

As Dr. Marie Puybaraud, global head of research at JLL Work Dynamics, says, "There is now an urgency to help corporate occupiers navigate what might be a long, complex, and demanding future of work transformation journey. There is no corporate roadmap to follow to manage the momentous challenges brought about by the pandemic. Organizations will need to heed the recovery in a responsible and agile way, empowering the workforce wherever they work."

## Learning from Hybrid Work Experimentation

Much can be learned from organizations that have embraced hybrid working. The experiences of other companies provide somewhat of a benchmark validating current strategies to inform the levers another organization may choose to pull in their strategies. Mobile apps, for example, are ideal for creating a differentiated experience for employees and visitors. Capital One's @work app, in particular, is worth noting because it goes well beyond space reservations or cafeteria menus, to include schedules that track shuttle progress, associate look-up, workplace service requests, and more. Also noteworthy, the company found creative ways to engage employees working at home during the pandemic, such as by providing curated chef menus with instructional cooking videos and mailing holiday theme boxes.

Organizations that are contemplating new campuses may want to consider what Microsoft is implementing at its Atlanta campus. Its commitment to diversity and inclusion is being brought to life with its investment in community development and future talent recruitment, providing a leadership template to be considered. Honeywell's Charlotte campus, with its digitized journey for every employee and integration with smart building concepts, suggest possibilities that other organizations could adopt while considering facilities upgrades and renovations.

Finally, Dell Technologies' Connected Workplace program provides a canvas of possibilities and a thought-provoking illustration of a workplace leader. The program is led by Mark Pringle, senior vice president of Corporate Real Estate, Global Facilities and EHS (environment, health, and safety) at Dell Technologies. To say that Pringle is a leader amongst leaders in the domain of workplaces would be an understatement.

> Dell has embraced flexible work for more than a decade, which made it easy to quickly pivot when the pandemic began. In 2013, after an initial three-year implementation of Connected Workplace, Dell established a goal to enable 50 percent of its workforce to work flexibly by 2020, at times in an office, but also from home and on the road.
>
> In the summer of 2020, Pringle was invited by the US Senate to describe the flexible workspace strategies that Dell has deployed and offer insight on ways that the federal government might integrate these strategies in the future. There he discussed the implications a flexible workplace approach might have for the need for physical office spaces and how Dell has approached these workspace strategies.
>
> Speaking to the Senate, Pringle said, "Before the onset of the pandemic, we had surpassed our goal, with approximately 65 percent of Dell Technologies employees leveraging work flexibility in their jobs – in the office just a couple of days a week – and 30 percent of our employees working remotely on any given day. Dell Technologies' Connected Workplace program encourages employees to design their ideal working arrangements, including remote work and flexible hours."

Pringle sees a marked shift in the workplace of the future. "Dell Technologies is redefining work not as a place or time, but an outcome," Pringle says of the Connected Workplace program. "Health and safety of the Dell Technologies family, our communities, and customers is our top priority. We see this as an opportunity to reinvent and redefine work in the new world and we are looking at ways to enable and innovate new ways of working with high levels of team member engagement and productivity. We are changing how we think about spaces, cybersecurity, meetings, travel, events, and policies, and we mustn't forget the ways employees find balance through their family, volunteer work, hobbies, and more. We need to evolve the dated mindset that being in an office full-time is an actual business imperative. Our objective is to create a stronger customer and team member experience by leveraging technology to unleash innovation and by being culturally committed to increasing our hybrid work style, focusing more on team member work-life balance, inclusion, flexibility, and choice.

"Our Connected Workplace program allows our employees to choose the work style that best fulfills their needs on the job and in life in a highly mobile, collaborative, and flexible work setting. The program has positively impacted our business, our approach to talent acquisition, and our environmental footprint."

Looking forward to the physical design of workplaces at Dell, Pringle plans on future offices with at least 70 percent collaboration space. "We will build more collaboration spaces, so that employees can work whenever and wherever they are most productive with a strong focus on the tools and technology that ensure a seamless team member experience and productivity."

Dell's visionary workplace transformation illustrates the new thinking today's reality requires. That is, a remote work policy alone is not the solution. As Pringle says about Connected Workplace, "This program is about a change in how we think about work – where work is not anchored to one place and time and instead is focused on outcomes."

Productivity proved to hold its own in the remote work setting when much of normal life was off-limits. Yet, doubts have emerged as to whether self-reported productivity really was the right measurement and whether full freedom of choice works in the long term.

This book argues that remote work can be a viable part of your workplace strategy – but it works best in the context of a holistic program focused on meeting employee needs and preferences. Remote work fits symbiotically alongside the recognition that the workplace is the beating heart of an organization, and that reality will not change.

This book has focused on the opportunity for organizations to invest in creating a boundaryless workplace that boosts productivity and advances talent and business strategies. We have explored the imperatives of culture; collaboration; sense of belonging, talent attraction, and retention; and differentiation that individuals and organizations alike are reassessing. The framework proposed here provides an organized approach that organizations can use to assess their particular environments and uncover their unique priorities. It can help organizations navigate a thoughtful path to creating the most effective workplace strategies backed by strategic workplace investments.

Workplace and work are inherently connected, but "workplace" is assuming entirely new meanings today. The pandemic forced workplace change, but organizations now have an opportunity to intentionally shape the purpose and characteristics of their workplaces. Taking action to get it right, right now, is how organizations can differentiate themselves, succeed, and win.

# ACKNOWLEDGMENTS

The evolution of ideas, products, technology, and services has been breathtaking over the last year. It has been an intense journey, especially since new learnings about new workplace concepts are emerging every day. And the process has taught us a lot. The power of collaboration – and the importance of digital technologies to enable it – has never been clearer.

A special thanks to our colleagues Marie Puybaraud, Robbie Hobbs, Caitlin McKenna, and Jen Hill, who have been essential partners in the journey. Led by Marcia Layton Turner, our list of collaborators is exhaustive and featured below. And thanks are due to Jennifer Harris, Michelle Pittman, and the team at Akrete Communications for their invaluable help. The most heartening experience for us has been the very responsive and enthusiastic participation of our collaborators as we've asked them to invest their time and energy in this project. We are grateful for their time, their ideas, and their patience.

- Dr. Andrea Chegut
- Andy Gloor
- Andy Poppink
- Becky Mikrut
- Benjamin Bader
- Chris Studney

- Christian Beaudoin
- Cynthia Kantor
- David Barnett
- Diane Hoskins
- Dan Ryan
- Elizabeth Brink
- Gayle Kantro
- Gina Barcal
- Greg O'Brien
- James Scott
- James Taylor
- Janet Pogue
- Jill Kouri
- John Gates
- Jordi Martin
- Julia Georgules
- Kevin Farley
- Kevin Wayer
- Kimberly Beal
- Lewis Woodward
- Mark Caskey
- Mark Gibson
- Mark Pringle
- Michael Dardick
- Michael Ford
- Natalie Engels
- Neil Murray
- Philip Ross
- Rajeev Chaba
- Rajesh Nambiar
- Ram Srinivasan
- Sandeep Sethi

- Scott Homa
- Stefanie (Stef) Spurlin
- Steve Brashear
- Steve Ramseur
- Sundar Nagarajan
- Susheel Koul
- Todd Burns
- Tom Carroll
- Traci Doane
- Vimal Kapur

# ABOUT THE AUTHORS

Dr. Sanjay Rishi is CEO, JLL Work Dynamics, for the Americas, and leads a team dedicated to helping organizations create, shape, and manage the future of work by enhancing the performance of their workplaces, real estate portfolios, and people. Rishi's team enables corporations and public institutions to create and maintain safer, more sustainable, and more inspiring workplace environments that blend human, digital, and experiential elements to facilitate innovation and creativity.

Rishi's career spans multiple industries and has been focused on technology-enabled transformation. As a partner with PricewaterhouseCoopers, and in various leadership positions at IBM, he led global businesses. Later, Rishi established and led IBM's Global Cloud Services business. In dual roles as chief information officer and chief strategy officer, Rishi led the digital transformation at Johnson Controls Automotive.

Rishi holds a PhD in management, a master's degree in management systems, and a bachelor of science degree in mechanical engineering. He currently serves on the board of the Chicago Council on Global Affairs.

Benjamin Breslau is chief research officer for JLL. He directs the overall activities of JLL's Research and Strategy team, sits on the JLL Americas Executive Committee, and chairs its Global Research Executive Board, guiding a 450-member global research department covering 100 countries. He oversees the delivery of the firm's leading research publications and services to occupier, investor, and institutional clients; presents JLL's thought leadership and research insights; and advises JLL and client leadership teams globally in the areas of real estate futures, strategy, and innovation.

Breslau has over 20 years in real estate economics and property research, is an active member of the Urban Land Institute, is on the executive board of the MIT Center for Real Estate, and holds a bachelor of science degree in economics, *magna cum laude*, from Emory University.

Peter Miscovich is a managing director who leads JLL's Strategy + Innovation consulting practice. With more than two decades of management consulting experience, Miscovich has pioneered multi-year research efforts focused upon the high-performance workplace and the "Future of Work." He has worked with Fortune 500 executive leadership teams in the management and execution of large complex client consulting engagements across multiple industry sectors.

As a former partner with PricewaterhouseCoopers, Miscovich has served in multiple senior leadership roles overseeing 1.5 billion square feet of corporate real estate transformation. He has led the development of multiple Fortune 100 Corporate Headquarters within the financial services, media, technology, telecommunications, and health care sectors.

Miscovich holds degrees from MIT (Massachusetts Institute of Technology) in enterprise transformation and human performance improvement and a bachelor of science degree in civil engineering from the University of Arizona. His academic research affiliations include Columbia University, Harvard University, and MIT. Miscovich serves on the Accenture Technology Vision Advisory Board and the CERES President's Council, and is an advisor to CoreNet Global, the Urban Land Institute, the World Economic Forum, and other leading organizations.

# INDEX

**A**

Acceleration point, 156
Accessibility, importance, 137
Activity-based design, 121–122
Activity-based spaces, impact, 122
Activity-based workplace design
    attributes, adoption, 49
Agile real estate portfolio, 183
Allen, Joseph, 87
Amenities, 124–126
    need, landlord understanding, 125
    novelty, 64
    private amenities, usage, 128
Anurag, Shagufta, 147
Anxiety, impact, 89, 166
Applications (apps), usage, 137–138
Artificial intelligence (AI), usage,
    135, 143–144
Augmented reality (AR), usage, 135, 189
AXA, health program, 88

**B**

Baby Boomers, impact, 27–29
Back-up power, monetization, 84
Bader, Benjamin, 47–48
Belonging
    culture, 71
    sense, importance, 70

Benioff, Marc, 77
Biometric identification systems,
    usage, 140
Biophilia, 127
BlackLine, employee assistance
    program, 88
Bloom, Nicholas, 50–51, 155, 158, 163
Brand experience, 71, 73
Branson, Richard, 63
Brashear, Steve, 186–188
Brink, Elizabeth, 115, 123, 124, 132
Brown, Ben, 57
Building technologies, health, 87–88
Built environment, heterogeneity, 146
Burnout, 54–55, 89, 114
*Bürolandschaft* (office landscape concept), 6
Business
    profitability (increase), happiness
        (impact), 90
    resiliency, importance, 69

**C**

Call centers/telesales, remote
    experiment, 59
Carbon Disclosure Project, 80–81
Central business districts (CBDs),
    10–12, 171
Chaba, Rajeev, 161

Change management, importance, 51
Chesky, Brian, 19
Chief human resource officers
        (CHROs), workplace role, 160
Choose-your-own-adventure
        workplace, 25
Cisco WebEx, 45
Clarke, Arthur C., 131
Cloud services, usage, 45, 168
Cloud technology, usage, 136
Cognitive fatigue, 114
Collaboration, 167
    skills, 173–175
Collaboration spaces, rethinking, 122–123
Company
    agile operating philosophy, 100
    culture, physical manifestation, 68
    worker-centric outlook, 72
Comte, Auguste, 26
Connected Workplace
        (Dell Technologies), 195–197
Consumer product development,
        basis, 24
Corporate offices, 6
    human experience, 113
Corporate real estate (CRE),
        153, 170
    cross-functional partnership, 51
    data-driven decision
        making, 175–176
    function, transformation, 158
    occupancy rates, impact, 48–49
    operations/business acumen, 175
    organizations, gaps, 83
    portfolio, 171–172
    teams, 143, 173–177
Corporate responsibility, 77
Corporate work week, change, 55
Creation, workplace
        (active center role), 123
Cube farms, 7, 113
Cubicles, 7–8
Culture, importance, 68

**D**
Dardick, Michael, 52, 122, 123
Data-driven space management, IoT
        devices (usage), 185
Data, impact, 135
De-densification, 56–57, 169
Dell, flexible work, 196–197
Demographics, destiny
        (equivalence), 26–27
Digital platform, usage, 162
Digital reservations, usage, 138
Digital space, experience, 131
Digital technologies, importance, 183
Digital twins, usage, 136, 185
Digital workplace, creation, 168–169
Digitization (Capital One), 133
Digitized workplace, arrival, 139–141
Distributed work, 52
Diversity, equity, and inclusion (DEI),
        79, 92–95, 185–186
    design, 124
    importance, 163–164
    initiatives, 85, 94
Diversity, meaning, 93
Dropbox, 45, 168
Drucker, Peter, 151

**E**
Ecosystem concept, organizational
        usage, 160–161
Employees
    confidence, feeling, 91
    engagement, 51, 71
    experience, 71, 110
    flexibility/choice, benefits, 159
    health, consideration, 91
    remote work option, 162
    study (*Workplace: Powered by Human
        Experience study*), 116
    survey, usage, 165
    voice, increase, 81
    workplace visitation frequency,
        management, 50

Employees, flexibility (offering), 47
Empowered housing, 93
Energy consumption, reduction, 84
ENERGY STAR certifications,
    usage, 81
Engels, Natalie, 120, 145, 148
Enterprise sustainability commitments,
    real estate (impact), 80
Environment
    complexity, determination,
        190, 191f, 192
    responsibility dimension, 79–86
Environmental quality solutions,
    impact, 85
Environmental, social, and governance
    (ESG), 77–78
    efforts, 83–84
    frameworks, resilience
        (incorporation), 102
    principles, 79
Environmental sustainability, 184–185
Equity, meaning, 93
Experience lover, 21
Experience metrics, identification,
    172–173
Experiential attributes, 117–129
Experiential workplace, 107, 108f
    elements, 186–189

**F**

Facebook, 163
    airplane hangar design, 8
Face-to-face activities/meetings/
    connections, 59, 75, 121,
        164, 170
Facility management, role, 83–84
Farley, Kevin, 80–81
Fast Followers, 192, 193f–194f
Feedback, impact, 193f–194f
Fink, Larry, 78
Flex, burnout, 53–54
Flex space, role (growth), 103
Ford, Michael, 34–35, 85, 95

Foster, Norman, 8
Frictionless access, 110
Friedman, Milton, 7

**G**

Gehry, Frank, 8
Gen Alpha, 26, 32
Gen Xers, 26–27, 29–30
Gen Yers, 29–30
Gen Zers, 26–27, 31–32
Gig economy
    on-demand labor, workforce
        flexibility, 102
    tapping, 37
Gloor, Andy, 14, 128
Google Drive, 45
Google, hybrid work model, 163
Google Meet, 45, 168
Googleplex, 8
Google Workspace, 168
GoSpace, AI usage, 144
Gratton, Lynda, 162
Great Recession, labor force
    reduction, 33
Greenhouse gas (GHG), reduction, 81, 84
Ground-floor retail, uniqueness, 125

**H**

Happiness, impact, 90
Health/wellbeing
    amenities, 126–127
    value, 184
Health/wellness
    responsibility dimension, 79, 86–92
    workplace/properties, impact, 87
*Healthy Building* (Allen/Macomber), 87
Hot-desk environment, adoption,
    166–167
HSBC, 163
Human cloud, impact, 102, 147
Human experience, 113, 116
    research/survey (JLL), 121–122
    strategy, defining, 166–169

Human resources (HR), 165
    cross-functional partnership, 51
    policies, 124
    real estate, relationship, 71
Hurst, Aaron, 67
HVAC, 57, 84, 128
Hybrid environment, challenges,
        145–149
Hybrid experiences, technology
        (impact), 148
Hybrid work
    experimentation, 195–198
    styles, approach, 174–175
Hybrid working, resilience
        (relationship), 103–104
Hybrid workplace, 47
    arrival, 139–141
    changes, 146–147
    ecosystem, 156, 160–161
    employee visitation frequency,
        management, 50
    growth, 44–53
    management, 171–172
    programs, basis, 53
    strategic framework, 181

I
Inclusion, 93, 148
In-demand talent, attraction, 124–125
Information technology (IT),
        cross-functional partnership, 51
Infrastructure, modernization, 57
In-house technology capabilities/
        collaboration, 146
Innovation
    culture, creation, 176–177
    location, 71
In-person collaboration, benefits, 122
In-person interactions,
        importance, 47–48
In-person meeting technology,
        usage, 138

In-person special events, plans, 52–53
Integrated workplace management
        system (IWMS), 143, 157f
Intelliflo, Zoom drop-ins, 88
Intelligent capabilities, impact, 147
Intelligent office, 132
Intelligent workplace
    arrival, 139–141
    defining, 133–137, 144
    digital capabilities, 134–137
    experience, 137–139
Internet-enabled network, usage, 134
Internet of Things (IoT), 86–88,
        134–135, 185, 188
Interstate system, impact, 11
Isolation feeling (reduction), shared
        experiences (usage), 92

J
Jobs, Steve, 1
Johnson & Johnson, wellbeing
        standards, 89

K
Kapur, Vimal, 110–111
Knowledge sharing, 35

L
Leaders, 192, 193f–194f
Learning
    location, 71
    programming, 123
Lease offerings, 52
LEED certifications, usage, 57, 81
Lego, corporate headquarters
        (playfulness), 9
Leidos headquarters, creation, 115
Liquid workforce, 15, 36–37, 102
Live-work-play environment, 125
Location-agnostic job opportunities,
        26
Location, alignment, 10–13

**M**

Macomber, John D., 87
Marketplace experience, 138
McCarty, Davis, 115
McLaurin, Janet Pogue, 127, 149
Median employee tenure (Employee
    Tenure Summary), 26
Mental health
    importance, 89
    mental wellbeing, Global Wellness
        Institute contrast, 89
Microsoft, 143
    digital leadership, 34–36
    spaceship headquarters, 8, 119
Microsoft Office, 167
Microsoft Teams, 33–34, 45, 168
    meetings, increase, 54
Millennials, 29–31
    Gen Xers, contrast, 30
    workforce percentage, 27
Miller, Herman, 6
Mixed-reality technologies, usage,
    189
Mobile apps, usage, 111
Morris, Ryan, 82

**N**

Nambiar, Rajesh, 45–46
Net zero carbon, approach/goals,
    84, 185
Next-generation intelligent
    technologies, usage, 131–132
Next-generation remote working,
    12–16
Nike
    brand experience, 73–74
    headquarters, embodiment, 9
Nomura, wellbeing program, 88–89

**O**

Occupancy costs, focus (change), 158
Occupancy rates, impact, 48–49

Offices
    action office, concept, 6–7
    activity-based design, 121–122
    density, factors, 190
    evolution, pandemic (impact),
        69–70
    have/have nots, division, 57
    homogeneity/blandness, 7
    landscape, concept, 6
    locations, movement, 55–58
    market, purpose, 74–75
    purpose, 48
    repair, opportunity, 149
    security, improvement, 119
    social hub, elimination (impact), 43
    space, ROI improvement, 164
    staff, buffer space (requirement), 56
    upgrades, funding opportunity, 170
    visitation time, desire, 42–43
    workers, experience, 66
    workspace, valuation, 23
Ohana Floors, 188
On-demand workplace options, 105
Open-plan offices, usage, 28, 35
OpenSpace, 132
Oracle, 143
Organizational priorities, 193f–194f
Organizational responsibility, 71
Outer urban environments, 12

**P**

Pandemic
    burnout, increase, 54
    company emergence, 15
    impact, 30, 64, 99, 114
Peak demand management,
    monetization, 84
People-centric workplace, 21–25,
    105, 142, 166
Performance
    anomaly analytics, usage, 84
    data, usage, 185

Personalized workplace, 1, 3f, 37–38, 142
  elements, 182–183
Peterson, Chris, 43
Physical health facilities, presence, 90
Physical objects, virtual
    representation, 136
Physical space, 6
  experience, 131
  transformation, 108
Physical workplace, changes, 80
Portfolio, resilience, 99
Post-Taylorism, 6
Pride, culture, 71
Pringle, Mark, 195–197
Private amenities, usage, 128
Product, 188
  development, iterative, 24–25
  flexibility, 2
Productivity, focus, 7
Profitability, focus, 7
Property technology (proptech), 144,
    146, 169, 189
  startups, global presence, 141
Propst, Robert, 6–7
Purpose-driven workplace, 67
Purpose, importance/value, 68–69
Puybaraud, Marie, 194

R
Real estate
  agile real estate portfolio, 183
  anthropological approach, 122
  assets, focus (change), 158
  decisions, 56–57
  human resources (HR),
      relationship, 71
  impact, 80
  location, importance, 187
  portfolio, optimization, 171–172
  solutions, impact, 141–145
  strategies, resilience
      (incorporation), 102

Remote communications technology,
    improvements, 45
Remote work
  adaptation, 33–34
  effectiveness, 13
  experience, 109
  flexibility, 163
  next-generation remote
      working, 12–16
  options, 58–59, 162
  policies, 14, 50
  popularity, 23–24
  productivity, 44
  worker preference, 42
Remote working, flexibility, 11–12
Resilience
  cooperation, requirement, 104–105
  definition, change, 101–103
Resiliency, 100–101
Responsible workplace, 63, 65f, 67–68
  elements, 183–186
Retirements, support, 28
Return on investment (ROI), 56
  office space ROI, improvement, 164
Ross, Phillip, 140, 168
Ryan, Dan, 144–145

S
Salesforce, 45, 163, 186–188
Salzberg, Sharon, 99
Santayana, George, 5
SAP, 143
Schultz, Howard, 113
Schwarzman, Stephen, 78
Scott, Robb, 115
Security, 119, 136–137
  policies, 167
Sellers, Robert, 93
Sick building syndrome, 104
Sinek, Simon, 53
Slack, 45, 162, 168
Smart building systems, usage, 142

Smart materials, usage, 134
Smith, Brad, 80
Social butterflies, space (creation), 128
Social distancing, 115, 169
Socialization, programming, 123
Socializing
   location, 71
   opportunity, loss, 72
Social wellbeing, importance, 91–92
Soft people skills, 174
Spurlin, Stefanie (Stef), 25, 44, 68,
   74, 126
Stakeholder capitalism, impact, 77
Stress, 89
Suburbia, value proposition, 11
Sustainability
   approaches, test, 85–86
   environmental sustainability,
      184–185
   initiatives, success, 83
   responsibility dimension, 79–86
   risk, 78

**T**
Talent
   nurturing, 60
   turnover, business risk, 102
Talent anywhere, workforce strategy,
   15
Task Force on Climate-Related Finan-
   cial Disclosures (TCFD), 102
Taylor, Frederick, 6, 113
Team-Based Spaces, Microsoft
   usage, 35
Technology
   importance, 46
   in-house technology capabilities/
      collaboration, 146
Telepresence robots, usage, 189
Touchless technology, usage, 137
Trust, formation, 53
Turntide Technologies, 141–142

**U**
Ulbrich, Christian, 41
Urban environment/living, 58
   employer return, 11
User experience (UX), 132–133

**V**
VergeSense, AI usage, 144–145
Virtual meeting technology, usage,
   138
Virtual reality (VR), usage, 135, 189
Voice-recognition technology,
   usage, 143

**W**
Wellbeing
   amenities, 126–127
   holistic wellbeing, employee
      experience, 127
   strategy, impact, 90
WELL certifications, 57
Wellness addict, 21
Wellness programming, basis, 127
Wheeler, Ben, 87–88
Whiteboarding, mirroring, 148
Work. *See* Remote work
   continuum, future, 49
   flexibility, 114–115
   future, 156, 157f, 165f
   hours, flexibility, 161
   hybrid work
      combinations, 44
      impact, 53–60
   options, 2
   spouse, term (usage), 114
   work marathon culture, creation,
      90
@work (Capital One app), 195
Work-at-home, employee
   test/usage, 46
Work.com platform, 187
Workday, 143

Workers
flexibility, 41–42
golden age, 71
in-person time, importance, 44
preferences (Workforce Barometer), 43
profiles, 22f
variation, 22–23
Workforce
energizing/inspiring, 109–110
flexibility, 102
liquid workforce, 15, 36–37, 102
resilience, 99
*Workforce Barometer* survey, 43, 54, 86
Work-from-home experiment, 13
Work-from-home hours, increase, 54
Work-from-home plans, popularity, 23
"Work from Home Pledge" (IBM), 115
Work-from-home policies, 167
Work-life balance, 29, 31, 53–54
Work-life flexibility, 44
*Workplace: Powered by Human Experience* (JLL research), 116, 117
Workplaces. *See* Intelligent workplace
activity-based workplace design attributes, adoption, 49
attributes, 118f
changes, 65
characterization, 2
choice/control, 20
collaboration technologies, usage, 45
company mission/purpose, alignment, 10
complexity, drivers, 191f
customer
appeal, 129
requirements, 24
data, usage, 144
definition, evolution, 68, 187
demographic shifts, impact, 64
design, evolution, 188

design/measurement/marketing, 3
ecosystem, 16, 51–52, 182
effectiveness, 20
engagement, 120
environments, opportunities, 28–29
equity/equality/meritocracy, 50
experience, 35, 132
leaders, power, 168
managers, impact, 173–177
experiential/social hubs, 32
experiential workplace, 107, 108f
factors, 82
first impressions, 117–120
flexibility, 8
function, changes, 72
future, 82
determination, 192–195
health/wellness focus, 86
hierarchy, reduction, 6
high-quality food service, delivery, 128
hospitality-driven changes, 74
humanization, 9–10
hybridization, 43, 45–46
hybrid workplace, growth, 44–53
innovation, 8–9
integrated workplace management system (IWMS), 143, 157f
investments, 169–170, 174
leaders, opportunities, 156
management, technologies (usage), 84–85
meaning, change, 198
model, emergence, 158–160
modes, 120
omnichannel approach, 139
on-demand workplace options, 105
optimization, 41
organizational culture/ priorities, 78–79
origin/evolution, 5

path, advancement, 152f
people-centric workplace, 21–25,
	105, 142, 166
personalization, 19
personalized workplace, 1, 3f
physical health facilities, presence, 90
priorities, 71, 160–165
productivity, approaches (test), 85–86
purpose, 70f
	change, 63–64, 69–70
purpose-driven workplace, 67
reimagining, 155
resilience, 99, 102
responsible workplace, 63,
	65f, 67–68
sensors, usage, 188
strategic decisions, 189–195

strategies, 5, 164, 174
technologies, impact, 45, 141
transformation, 72, 79, 108, 177, 192
Workspace
	allocations, 165f, 169
	options, 166–167
World Economic Forum (Davos),
	responsibility dimension, 78
Worst-case scenarios, debate, 100–101

**Y**
Young parents, job worries, 33

**Z**
Zoom, 162, 168
	drop-ins (Intelliflo), 88
Zoom-a-thon, impact, 33–34